LEARNING TO LEARN AND THE NAVIGATION OF MOODS

The Meta-Skill for the Acquisition of Skills

LEARNING TO LEARN AND THE NAVIGATION OF MOODS

The Meta-Skill for the Acquisition of Skills

Gloria P Flores

ISBN-13: 9780692801796
ISBN-10: 0692801790

Foreword

Back in 1980, what has come to be known as "the Dreyfus Skill Model" made its first appearance in a report on skill acquisition in the training of pilots that we (Hubert and Stuart) prepared for the US Air Force. Although our preferred way of formulating the five or six different stages has evolved over the years, one thing has remained unchanged: our conviction that emotional engagement is essential to progressing up the ladder of skill acquisition. Put simply, in order for us to acquire new skills, it has to matter to us how well we are doing in our learning. If we are indifferent to making mistakes and failing to improve, we will not be receptive to what we can *learn* from making mistakes. Feeling bad about doing poorly and feeling good about doing well are extremely important for improving at the skill you are learning.

But being vulnerable to such emotional vicissitudes can be discouraging to the learner. Feeling bad about doing poorly and failing to advance can often cause learners to hold back from taking risks and striving to improve, stalling them at being an advanced beginner or merely competent.

Gloria Flores's work on learning to learn expands upon our work by further elaborating on the kinds of affective responses, what she calls *moods*, that can show up in each stage of learning (for example, frustration, arrogance, perplexity, ambition, and confidence, to name a few). Many of these emotions may lead to an interruption or abandonment of learning if we are not prepared to recognize and deal with them.

Someone averse to failure and the negative emotions and moods it can produce will not advance beyond mere competence. Although such stalling
and copping out is a side-effect predicted and described by the Skill Model,
in our subsequent work on skill acquisition, we have not pursued the question of how an emotionally engaged learner can navigate and cope with the
emotional ups and downs that always come along with learning something
new. Gloria's account of the role of moods in learning provides an important
missing link between a descriptive insistence upon emotional engagement in
learning and a guide for actively coping with the challenging vicissitudes such
emotional engagement will involve.

The essay below is full of examples of learners succumbing to emotional
blocks on their path of learning, whether it is a young child who gives up on
learning math, or the media consultant who gives up on learning to play the
computer game being used in a teamwork training exercise. Given the emotional dynamics of learning, it is all too easy for a learner to fall into a negative mood like resignation or impatience. Such moods are ways in which the
necessary emotional engagement of the learner ironically gets in the way of
her learning.

One of the key contributions of this essay is the taxonomy of moods that are
typically involved in learning a new skill. Together with the account of how one
can move out of moods that are obstacles to learning into the ones that are
conducive to learning, this taxonomy of moods reveals a path for the learners
to become more receptive to what their moods reveal about the progress of
their learning process. Such increased sensitivity to the revelatory dimensions
of moods can enable learners to use their moods to help them reflect on their
learning process, thereby empowering them to propel forward in their learning rather than to submit to emotional vulnerabilities and give up.

In this way learners can develop the "meta-skill" for acquiring skills. This
meta-skill involves abilities to become aware of the moods one falls into while
learning, to see what perhaps unrealistic or ungrounded expectations and

assessments these moods reveal, and to cultivate moods conducive to learning, like resolution and ambition.

In the second half of her essay, Gloria usefully extends the original skill model by transposing it into the social dimension. Our skill model was originally couched in terms of skills that an individual executes mostly on his or her own, situations in which interactions with others are relegated largely to a strategic plane, for example, flying a jet aircraft, driving a car, or playing chess. But the skill model is expanded here to illuminate the acquisition of skills that are *essentially social* skills: skills for the coordination of cooperative group action. The emotional challenges of learning are more intensely involved in skills that have to do with working and coordinating with other people, since now we are dealing not only with the ups and downs of our own involvement, but also those that are bound to emerge in the face of the way others treat us and succeed or fail to live up to our expectations and standards. Given the extra challenges involved in learning such social skills, the work that Gloria has done here will be an important contribution to every one of us who has to coordinate with other people, which is to say, every one of us. This is why we recommend that this essay be closely read and its contents widely reflected and acted upon.

Stuart E. Dreyfus, Hubert L. Dreyfus, and B. Scot Rousse

Second Foreword

I teach computer operating systems to adult graduate students. Operating systems are a difficult technology to master and it is easy for students to fall into unproductive moods while studying them. Many times in the past, my students have not been able to escape their unproductive moods and have wound up getting poor grades and being dissatisfied with the course.

Gloria Flores's insight into moods as an unseen force that can either support or block learning is a breakthrough for educators. If you are not aware of your own moods, all you can see is that you were able to learn this but not that, but you cannot explain why you were able to learn this but not that. To help students learn, therefore, as a teacher I need to learn how to show them how to recognize their moods, and even better teach them how to shift to productive moods.

In this writing, Gloria Flores points out that young children tend to dwell in productive moods, for they are ever eager to learn new things. By their teen years, sometimes much earlier, many have changed: they seem to frustrate easily, fear mistakes, and distrust their abilities. In these moods they get defensive and resist learning. She points out that adults fall into learning-blocking moods as well. For example, adult experts are confident about their abilities, but when thrust into a situation where they need to learn something new, many quickly become uncomfortable and lose their confidence. They do not welcome the opportunity to learn something new; they want to escape. Their moods of confusion, anxiety, insecurity, embarrassment, and resignation

block their professional development and advancement. Their long expertise left them rusty at cultivating the positive attitudes of beginners – being
okay with not knowing something, allowing themselves time to learn, or asking for help – and prone to worrying about their reputation if others see them
as not competent. In reading Gloria Flores's account, I realized that one of
a teacher's greatest contributions is to help students recognize their moods
and learn to shift to moods productive for learning.

These insights helped recently with a cohort of adult (age 30-35) graduate
students in my operating systems class. They were enjoying the class until
their first quiz. Many of them did not get the grades they thought they de-
served and fell into various bad moods including discouragement, anger, and
even resentment. Inspired by Gloria Flores's insights, I decided not to talk to
them about the quiz's answers, but instead about their moods. I composed a
poetic page that walked through all the moods a beginner is likely to experience. I called it "The Beginner's Creed." The text is as follows:

> I am a beginner.
> I am entering a new game about which I know nothing.
> I do not yet know how to move in this game.
> I see many other people playing in this game now.
> This game has gone on for many years prior to my arrival.
> I am a new recruit arriving here for the first time.
> I see value to me in learning to navigate in this domain.
> There is much for me to learn:
> The basic terminology
> The basic rules
> The basic moves of action
> The basic strategies
> While I am learning these things I may feel various negative reactions:
> Overwhelmed at how much there is to learn
> Insecure that I do not know what to do
> Inadequate that I lack the capacity to do this
> Frustrated and discouraged that my progress is so slow
> Angry that I have been given insufficient guidance

Anxious that I will never perform up to expectations on which my career depends
Embarrassed that everyone can see my mistakes
But these moods are part of being a beginner. It does not serve my goal and ambition to dwell in them. Instead,
If I make a mistake, I will ask what lesson does this teach.
If I make a discovery, I will celebrate my aha! moment.
If I feel alone, I will remember that I have many friends ready to help.
If I am stuck, I will ask for help from my teachers.
Over time, I will make fewer mistakes.
I will gain confidence in my abilities.
I will need less guidance from my teachers and friends.
I will gain familiarity with the game.
I will be able to have intelligent conversations with others in the game.
I will not cause breakdowns for promises that I lack the competence to keep.
I have an ambition to become competent, perhaps even proficient or expert in this game. But for now,
I am a beginner

Upon entering the classroom after that quiz, I saw a sea of dejected faces and downcast eyes. I asked them, "How many of you are an expert in some area?" Every hand went up. Then I asked, "How many of you feel like a beginner in operating systems?" Every hand went up. Then I asked, "How many of you *like* being a beginner?" Only two hands went up. I said, "We need to have a conversation about that."

I handed out the Beginner's Creed and asked them to read it. When they had finished, I read it aloud so that I could intonate its moods. I asked them to read it to themselves every day for a week. For the rest of the course, the students were much more relaxed about their roles as beginners and were much more engaged in the work of the course. At the end of the course, when the project teams stood up to make their final presentations to the class, one team said proudly, "We are beginners! And look at what we have accomplished!" In my concluding remarks for the course, I said, "Congratulations. You are now all advanced beginners. You are prepared to learn to be competent with operating systems." Some smiled with pride.

What is even more interesting is that the Beginner's Creed resonated with concerns my students had outside of class and in other departments of the university. After reading the Creed, one student immediately asked, "May I give a copy of this to my son?" Another asked the same question regarding his boss. The Senior Marine officer on campus showed it to one of the students who was having a particularly hard time acclimating to his studies; the student said, "I wish you had given me this when I first arrived! I see that I have been resisting too much." The campus librarian framed a copy and hung it on the wall of the library. Gloria Flores's insight is powerful indeed and speaks to a yearning that many people have been unable to articulate.

I dedicate the Creed to Gloria Flores and her insights about the effects of moods on students' learning.

Peter J. Denning

Preface

There is much to say about learning, and much has been said in numerous books and papers by scholars of education. I am not a scholar, but I have had the opportunity to work closely with many people as they learned how to do something they were unable to do before. I've observed, over and over again, how people learn new skills, and how often – despite their best efforts – they encounter *emotional learning stumbling blocks* that hinder their learning.

I am a lawyer by training, but have spent most of my career helping people develop skills to work more effectively in teams. I focus on enabling people to acquire not only intellectual understanding, but also the ability to perform activities in a particular domain that they could not have performed before. Certainly, when we first embark on a learning process we need to learn basic rules, to receive instructions, and to orient ourselves to standard practices, but my interest and attention has been on how we cultivate new skills.

With this focus, for more than seven years my colleagues and I have delivered a course called Working Effectively in Small Teams, aka WEST. We've worked with people from many countries, wide-ranging professions, assorted age groups, and various types of organizations, such as Fortune 500 companies, universities, the armed forces, small companies, start-ups, and solo practitioners. We help participants develop or improve skills that enable them to work more effectively in teams. For example, participants develop:

- The ability to coordinate their commitments with others.
- The ability to learn from each other and to listen for concerns by making and exploring assessments.
- The ability to build trust.
- The ability to cultivate the emotional fortitude to cope with change, disturbance, or the unknown on an ongoing basis.

We assign reading materials and lead conversations in which we present a rich theoretical framework for how human beings communicate. We also lay out the actions needed to work more effectively in teams. Yet even though our students understand the framework, and desire to learn new skills, they often stumble.

For example, a senior manager of a large Fortune 100 company wanted to learn how to delegate tasks effectively. She tended to do much of the work by herself, but when it came time to ask members of her team to do something, she could not bring herself to do it. She understood that it was important for her to delegate more to her team and knew that she could make requests of people. She certainly wanted to, and was motivated to learn to delegate because she thought it would greatly benefit her. Among other things, she was convinced that it would allow her: (1) to focus on things at work that she currently did not have time to focus on; (2) to leave earlier and not have to work every weekend figuring things out that she didn't know how to do; and (3) to spend a bit more time with her family. However, when the opportunity came for her to delegate during an exercise, she quickly dismissed any desire she had to learn to delegate more, and continued her pattern of doing things all on her own. When asked if she considered asking for help and delegating responsibilities – the subject of a recent class reading assignment – she acknowledged that while the exercise had provided her the perfect opportunity for her to have done so, but she could not do it. Something got in her way and she was not predisposed to take the action that she knew, in theory, was possible for her to take. Upon reflection, she could see that she had fallen into the following unproductive moods about learning to delegate:

- Frustration – I want to be able to delegate but I can't;
- Resignation – asking others to do something that I can do or should be able to do is not possible; and
- Insecurity – if I ask for help, it means I am incompetent to do something by myself and others will begin to see me as the "weakest link" on the team.

As a result, although she knew that she could delegate, she did not perceive that move as a possibility. She thought she should not ask for help. Working with her, and many other people with whom we have had the pleasure of working, we have repeatedly witnessed this phenomenon: people want to learn a new skill, but for some reason they cannot take the actions they need to take to learn. A few more examples:

- A vice-president of sales who wanted to learn to build a strong team. Yet, whenever his team did not live up to his expectations, instead of taking action that could grow his team's competence and enable them to do things better next time, he just did the work himself. He put aside his goal of building a strong team, and he found himself in moods of impatience and frustration. His moods did not let him see actions he could take, such as new practices he could implement or conversations that he could have with members of his team that would advance him toward the goal of building a strong team. *I wish I could rely on my team, but it's a waste of time to do so. The work finds its way back to me in the end. I should just do the work by myself.*
- A senior consultant who wanted to learn to negotiate her commitments better and to say no when she needed to. She found herself overwhelmed with commitments, many of which she thought she should not do, but when the opportunity arose to say no, she found that she could not utter that word. Saying no was not appropriate to her. She thought that others would be offended, and would think less of her. *I don't want them to think that I am not committed to the team. I should not say no.* She fell into resignation about the possibility of

ever being able to say no, and resented her teammates asking her to do something that she did not have the time for.

- A senior consultant who was transitioning to becoming an entrepreneur and wanted to learn to make effective offers. When the opportunity arose for him to make an offer to his colleagues that would have been quite useful for their team, he did not. He could not. Instead, he stayed quiet. He was in a mood of frustration because he wanted to be able to make offers, but thought it was inappropriate for him to act like he knew something others did not. *They are all smart people. Who am I to assume that I know more than they do? I shouldn't make an offer.*

All of these people wanted to develop an ability to do something: to delegate, to build trust, to build a stronger team, to negotiate and say no when necessary, to work in teams, to make offers, and so forth. They understood intellectually what actions they could take and what they needed to do, but when they found themselves in situations where they could practice taking the necessary action, they could not. Their emotional disposition in those moments held them back from doing so.

These *emotional learning stumbling blocks* can trip us up at any age, if we are not alert to them. During the same time period that my colleagues and I have been delivering WEST, I have been busy raising three boys, and learning about learning from them as well. As a mom, I have been fascinated by how quickly young children can go from being confident, persistent, and motivated about their studies to feeling insecure, confused, resigned, and unengaged with the material. One moment one of my sons liked math and thought that he was good at it, and the next moment, after encountering a problem that he found challenging and could not understand right away, he was ready to give up on math because he was "stupid" at it. At the ripe old age of 10, he declared that he was not interested in studying anything that required mathematics because he was bad at it. He was willing to shut the door on countless possibilities because all of a sudden he perceived himself as "stupid" in math.

I saw this story repeat itself with all three of my sons. The same son quit draw-ing because he did not see how he could get better when he began to per-ceive that others were better than he was. *If I am not the best at it, I should not do it anymore. It's not good to do things if others are going to think that you are bad at it.* Another son really enjoyed writing until fourth grade, and then he was asked to write a structured five-paragraph essay for the first time, and his love of writing, along with his confidence, greatly diminished. He had not yet learned how to do an essay where he had to write a thesis statement, provide supporting evidence, and write a conclusion, but instead of getting instructions from his teacher or asking for help so that he could learn to write this kind of essay, he fell into a bad mood about not knowing how to do it, which made learning much harder for him. *Writing is hard. I am bad at it. I hate it. I don't understand it. I don't want to do it. I am stupid.*

Rather than enjoying the possibility of learning something new, my kids, like others I have known, sometimes fell into unproductive moods.

- They fell into confusion, where not knowing showed up as something bad.
- They fell into resignation, where they did not see anything they could do to learn the subject at hand, or to get better at it.
- They fell into insecurity, and not only questioned their ability to learn but were sure that others would think of them as less smart because they did not know.
- They fell into impatience, and expected themselves to "get it" quickly; if they did not, that meant that they were not smart and would never be able to understand the subject matter in question.
- They were frustrated with themselves, with their teachers, with me, and with the learning process in general.

Instead of embracing the unknown as an opportunity to discover and to grow, young children often feel bad about not knowing how to do something, and want to run away and quit. "You don't understand," each of my boys has said to me at some point when I've tried to help with a homework assignment. "There is nothing I can do about this."

In those moments, there was nothing I could do to help them understand the material in question. They simply were unable to listen to me. They were not able to learn. Those moments were a catalyst to my learning about learning. How we learn to learn became a question that perplexed and intrigued me, as I became convinced that this skill was essential for embracing the unknown and for being able to learn for the rest of our lives. This was a skill that I wanted my children to develop.

Thankfully, my work world and my family world intersected at this time. I realized that what was happening to my children was not unique to them; nor was it unique to the people who participated in our courses. As they embarked on the process of learning something new, it was not uncommon for them to fall into moods that were not conducive to learning – such as confusion, arrogance, impatience, frustration, insecurity and resignation – and unless they were able to overcome them, they were not predisposed to take the kinds of action needed for them to be able to continue to learn – like practicing, making mistakes, and asking for help. If they were unable to shift out of those unproductive moods, their ability to learn was blocked.

Consequently, an essential element of learning to learn is opening up emotional dispositions that prompt us to take effective action. Instead of giving in to our desire to quit, we can engage in a process of reflection and practice where we learn to cultivate alternative emotional dispositions that will imbue us with the will to continue practicing, taking risks, asking for help, and learning. Fortunately, just as there are moods that hinder our learning, there are others that predispose us to take the kinds of actions we need to take to continue to learn. If we are in a mood of wonder, for example, ignorance shows up as a new frontier to explore, not as something to be embarrassed by. If we are in a mood of ambition, an obstacle shows up as a hurdle to overcome, not as another reason for giving up, which is what happens in a mood of resignation.

Learning is a process and it requires time. And, as Professors Stuart and Hubert Dreyfus of the University of California at Berkeley assert in their Skill Acquisition Model, a person who embarks on the process of acquiring a new skill will pass through different stages of competence, starting as a beginner and ending as a master. Drawing on their work, I could not only see that people could be expected to have different performance abilities depending on their stage of learning, but I could also begin to see a pattern in the moods that learners routinely fell into at each stage. For example, it is not uncommon for a beginner to fall into confusion (*I don't understand what is going on and I don't like it!*) and insecurity (*I am never going to get it. Maybe I am not smart enough to do this*), and if they are unable to shift out of these moods, they will diminish the likelihood of allowing themselves to continue to learn. If a learner has reached a higher level of competency, such as the stage the Dreyfus brothers call "competent" – where the person feels responsible for results but does not have much experience and is by no means an expert – she or he will very possibly fall into a mood of being overwhelmed. Unless a person at this stage of learning is able to cultivate a mood of self-confidence and/or is able to get help from others, she or he may decide to quit as the stress can begin to feel unbearable.

We don't get to control what moods we fall into. Our culture and life experiences trigger them automatically. Sometimes we will find ourselves in unproductive moods. That's normal. We can, however, learn to navigate our moods and shift out of the ones that get in the way of our learning. If we aspire to continue to learn, this ability is essential at any stage of the learning process. Once we develop the ability to navigate our moods, our ability to learn other skills is greatly enhanced. Hence, I see the navigation of moods as the meta-skill for acquiring other skills.

The process of active reflection and practice that I share in the following pages has proven helpful to the people I have had the privilege to accompany as they endeavored to learn and cultivate an emotional predisposition that would allow them to overcome stumbling blocks along the way. This process has proven useful to me as well. In fact, the genesis of this book was a compilation of notes that I originally made for myself as I learned to guide others through the learning process. Instead of quitting whenever I felt like I hit a wall and could not make the progress I wanted to make, I was able to take a step back and take the actions I needed to take to continue to learn.

I hope the reader finds it helpful too.

Acknowledgments

Many people helped with this book by giving me their comments, by making edits, by discussing this topic with me, and by inspiring me.

First, I have to include every person who has participated in our Working Effectively in Small Teams experiment over the last seven years who gave me the privilege to witness their learning process which in turn allowed me to learn. I am humbled by their openness, perseverance, and commitment to continue to learn whether they are 25 or 90. At the end of every course I reflect on my learning and I can honestly say that I learned just as much, if not more, than the participants. They have enabled me to grow as a person and as mentor to our clients, and also as a mother and mentor to my children.

Along with the participants, I want to thank two people who have been instrumental in the delivery of this course since day one: my sister, Javiera Flores, and Juan Bulnes. I could not have done it without them. Dick Babillis joined our team shortly after taking the course himself and has been an endless resource for us, and for me in particular. In addition, I want to thank Peter Luzmore for being my partner in designing and delivering the first pilot version of this course. If Peter had not held my hand in the early days, I would not have ventured into the world of role-playing games as confidently as I did.

Numerous others provided unwavering support, many conversations, countless reviews, edits, and suggestions. Of these, my sister Maria Fernanda Flores,

B. Rousse, and Dick Babillis stand out, but I also want to thank Larry Fisher, Peter Denning, Ron Kaufman, Michele Gazzolo, George West, Fred Disque, Pedro Rosas, Veronica Vergara, Chris Wiesinger, Pablo Flores, Rodolfo Larrea, Bill Fine and Salim Premji for taking the time to read earlier versions of this book and for providing constructive feedback.

I would also like to thank Hubert Dreyfus and Stuart Dreyfus for creating the Skill Acquisition Model in 1980. Their work inspired me to explore the successful navigation of the learning process from beginner to mastery. I also want to thank them for meeting and discussing this book with me. And in particular, I would like to thank Stuart Dreyfus for continuing to make reading recommendations.

In addition, I want to thank my mother, Gloria Letelier, for always encouraging me to write and to share my writing with others. I have written many documents over the years, and without her encouragement, many would sit on my hard drive to be shared only with my colleagues or in our courses. Similarly, I would like to thank her "twin" when it comes to encouraging me to write and to act, my husband, Bill Fine. Whenever I fall into self-doubt (*Who am I, a non-academic, to be talking about learning?*), my husband finds a way to steer me away from insecurity towards self-confidence.

I also want to thank my three children, Fernando, Benji, and Lucas for always inspiring me, for teaching me how to learn every day, and for patiently providing me with in-game support countless times.

And last, but definitely not least, I want to thank my father, Fernando Flores, for being the person he is, and for inspiring me to learn. Almost everything that gave rise to this book would not have been possible had he not opened the space for me to play, to explore, and to learn alongside him. His work on moods and how human beings work together was a springboard for my thinking and the work that I have been doing for much of my adult life. A generous mentor, he has mastered the art of learning to learn. I hope that when I am his age, I will still be busy doing the same.

1

Introduction – Learning to Learn

Many of us agree that one of the most important skills we need to develop for ourselves and for our children is the skill of learning to learn. A quick overview of the press and the business literature highlights "learning to learn" as a crucial skill.[1]

---

1 See John Bennett, emeritus associate dean/professor, University of Connecticut: "The most important skill for everyone to learn is how to learn!" ("Ten Skills Every Student Should Learn," eSchool News, August 11, 2011.) See also Thomas Friedman, author of numerous books and columnist for *The New York Times*, who over ten years ago suggested that we need to "learn to learn" and warns that "what we learn today in school will be outdated by tomorrow, and therefore, the most successful people in the 'flat world' will be those who can adapt and learn quickly. The greater our curiosity and passion for learning, the greater chances we will have for success later in life" (*The World is Flat: A brief history of the 21st Century*. New York: FSG Books. Copyright 2005). In 2014, Friedman wrote about hiring practices at Google, where Laszlo Bock, the person in charge of hiring, told him that the top "hiring attribute" they look for in a new hire is "general cognitive ability, not I.Q. It's learning ability" ("How to Get a Job at Google," New York Times. February 22, 2014).

But what is this "ability" to learn? How do we define it, never mind acquire it? Recognizing the importance of this ability, many HR Consultants advise job candidates to show that they are "willing to learn" in their resumes. See Randall S. Hansen and Katherine Hansen's "What Do Employers *Really* Want? Top Skills and Values Employers Seek from Job-Seekers," where they advise job seekers to show that they are "enthusiastic, knowledge hungry [learners], eager to meet challenges and [able to] quickly assimilate new concepts." For another example, see Boris Groysberg's article in the *Harvard Business Review*, "Keep Learning Once You Hit the C-Suite," where he writes about what skills companies prize in C-level executives, and mentions that the terms "flexible," "adaptable," and "curious" came up frequently – all characteristics that we can group together with the general skill of being good at learning to learn. One consultant described a typical in-demand executive as "a sponge," primed to "take in new skills" and "learn from the people around [her]." Another endorsed a "willingness to learn and adapt to changing environments," and a third urged "adaptability, the ability to operate in multi-cultural environments and the openness to learn."

A Google search of "learning to learn" produces 855,000,000 hits in less than half a second. The European Union has identified learning to learn as a key competence for "continuing to gain employment and [being] included within everyday life activities including those of civil society and decision making."[2] The World Economic Forum has stated that given the challenges professionals confront in today's world, "life-long learning is more critical than ever."[3] Learning to learn has been defined in many different ways, including "the ability to pursue and persist in learning,"[4] and as the "ability and willingness to adapt to novel tasks, activating one's commitment to thinking and the perspective of hope by means of maintaining one's cognitive and affective self-regulation in and of learning action."[5] Nevertheless, despite the widespread recognition that learning to learn is a crucial skill for us to master, there is no consensus on how to define it, nor is there much guidance for how to develop it. Drawing on years of training, experience and observing people learning new skills, I attempt in this book to contribute to an understanding of how one can learn to learn.

But why do we need to develop this skill? Are we not born with the capacity to learn? We learn to talk, walk, and use the potty without having to learn how to learn first. Young children have a great capacity to learn, but for some reason, it seems to deteriorate over time, often much sooner than we would expect. As the mother of three kids, I never cease to be surprised when I hear young children say that they are not going to pursue some field of study because they stink at math, or because they are not "good writers." They are hardly out of diapers, and they are already closing the door on a wide range of disciplines and potential careers. One of my sons, who routinely had a sketchpad handy and who used to draw all of the time when he was younger, stopped drawing all of a sudden at the age of 10. I was surprised and disappointed because I thought, as his unbiased mother of course, that he was quite good at it. I asked him why he was not drawing, as I really liked

---

2 Bryony Hoskins and Ulf Fredriksson, *Learning to Learn: What Is It and Can It Be Measured?* (in JRC Scientific and Technical Reports, 2008), 11.
3 Nikias, C.L. Max, "What will the future of education look like?" (*World Economic Forum*)
4 The European Union's definition. (*Learning to Learn: What Is It and Can It Be Measured?*, 12.)
5 The University of Helnsinski's definition. (Id., 18.)

his work, and he said, "I am not that good. There are people who are better than me so I don't really feel like drawing anymore." Despite my encouragement, he steadfastly refused to draw at all unless he had to as part of a school assignment.

Why does this happen? The short answer is: life happens. Starting at a young age, we begin to acquire standards that guide our behavior by helping us to judge what is appropriate or not appropriate. Our families, our friends, our teachers, our chosen field of study, our professions, our colleagues, our culture – intentionally or unintentionally – all influence how we see the world and what we think is okay to do or not to do. We begin to acquire a lot of "shoulds" – what we should do or not do, what we should be able to do, or what we should know, among others. This is to be expected, and there is nothing wrong with it – it is part of being a person in the world with others. In fact, this process has historically helped us become part of and thrive in our respective communities, communities bound by certain shared standards. However, the standards of behavior that we come to adhere to may have the unintended consequence of closing us off to learning.

My colleagues and I have seen this negative side effect of misplaced standards first-hand in delivering the services of our companies. Through our experience working with adults for many years[6] – and quite a few children

---

6 I have had the honor and privilege of observing and participating in the learning process of many people. During the past seven years, my colleagues and I have worked with hundreds of people through our company, Pluralistic Networks, Inc. The company is focused on enabling people to develop skills to work more effectively with others, in teams, and in what we call pluralistic networks, which are networks of people from different backgrounds, different cultures, etc., but that collaborate with one another with respect. The skills that we focus on helping our clients acquire include, among others, the ability to coordinate commitments, build trust, listen and make offers that add value to others, observe and manage moods, lead effective teams with shared purpose, and, most importantly, to learn. Prior to Pluralistic Networks, we operated Business Design Associates (BDA), a management consulting company, where we worked with thousands of individuals, including many top executives and their staff, from large corporations throughout Europe and the Americas, including companies in New York, Boston, Canada, Mexico, Chile, Italy, Sweden, France, and Switzerland.

too[7] – we have been able to observe over and over again how standards of behavior that we have committed to, and which may be helpful to us in some settings, may not serve us well when it comes to learning. In my son's case, he was committed to being the best at drawing, and to doing it as long as he was the "best." When he realized that there are other people who he thought drew better than him, and that he was not the "best," he no longer wanted to pursue that endeavor. The possibility of continuing to practice, learning new techniques, taking courses from experts, and so on, did not even enter his mind. Even though he was only 10, if he was not the best, he believed he needed to abandon that activity, which until then had seemed like something he enjoyed and dedicated quite a bit of time to.

This tendency to abandon an activity due to the application of a misplaced or overly severe standard is not limited to the growing pains of childhood or adolescence. It is a widespread human phenomenon. At the other end of the age spectrum, my colleagues and I have worked with many adults who are considered "experts in their fields" and who, in time, have come to value themselves under the identity of being the experts who know the answers and who can tell people what to do. Yet, when they find themselves in situations where they are beginners themselves, they don't seize the opportunity to learn something new. They are blocked by their prior commitment to the standard of being an expert, a standard which might appropriately guide them in their area of expertise, but which is misplaced when they must learn a skill at which they are initially bound to be just a beginner, someone who by definition can't expect himself or herself to know what to do without guidance. In other words, a beginner cannot possibly expect to meet the standards of an expert. Yet, we often observe experts in their professions, who despite intellectually comprehending that they are beginners at something become embarrassed, quiet, and disengaged when placed in a situation where they are no longer experts. Instead of asking for guidance and being open to the learning process that all beginners must go through, they feel anxious and

---

7 We have worked with our own sons and daughters, nephews and nieces, as well as indirectly with children in the Altamira school in Chile, a school owned by Fernando Flores and other family members.

stressed, and often shy away from the new activity, assessing, for example, that in this situation they better just stay out of the way.[8]

If left unexamined, the standards that normally guide our behavior can limit our ability to learn. We might be reluctant to put ourselves in situations where we will be beginners who don't have a clue what to do, or where we need to ask for help, or where we need to take risks and make mistakes as part of the learning process. Learning to explore our assessments and their underlying standards is a key aspect of learning to learn. Of course, this is easier said than done, but with recurrent practice, we can learn, and learning to learn can itself become a higher-order skill, a skill for acquiring skills.

---

8 In "Teaching Smart People How to Learn," Chris Argyris writes that smart people are often the worst learners. Perhaps, he speculates, "...because many professionals are almost always successful at what they do, they rarely experience failure. And because they have rarely failed, they have never learned how to learn from failure" (*Harvard Business Review* May-June 1991). Consequently, when they are criticized or don't do well in something, they get embarrassed and defensive, and tend to blame others and shut down. They are not open to learning.

I agree with late Professor Argyris that a mood of defensiveness can shut down learning. It will also shut down our ability to listen to the other people or to collaborate with them. This does not happen only to top management consultants, the people Professor Argyris focused on in his article, but to many people, from all walks of life, whether or not they have experienced failure. Professor Argyris argued that people can be taught to break the cycle of defensive reasoning by learning to "reason productively," including learning to recognize the reasoning they use when they design and implement their actions. I agree that people can be taught to break the cycle of defensive reasoning, but propose that what can be taught is broader than that. I will say more about this later in this book, but for now suffice it to say that a mood of defensiveness is one of several moods that can routinely shut down learning. A mood of defensiveness often shows up when we hear what we interpret as criticism about our performance and our automatic assessment is something like "this person is attacking me. I have to defend myself by explaining why I am right or why others are to blame." A possible standard underneath this assessment is that "one must be right at all times or else others will think that I am not smart/competent/worthy of being part of the team," and hence we automatically defend ourselves. Other moods, such as arrogance, insecurity, confusion, or anxiety, can shut down learning as well. If we can learn to identify these moods when we find ourselves in them, and to shift them so that we can open ourselves up to continue learning, we will be well on our way to reaching our learning objectives, whatever these may be. Learning to navigate our moods – shifting away from unproductive ones and cultivating ones that are more conducive to continued learning – is a skill that can benefit everyone, from 50 year-old senior executives to 10 year-old children.

In a world where uncertainty and rapid change are the norm, where we cannot control changes in technology, regulations, or the environment, but where we need to cope and navigate with these on an ongoing basis, learning to learn appears all the more as an essential skill we are called to cultivate.

2

What Gets In The Way of Learning

Starting at a young age, we develop standards of behavior to help us navigate the communities in which we participate – our families, our schools, our professions, and our culture as whole. We judge certain behaviors as appropriate or inappropriate according to these standards. As a mother, I have had the opportunity to repeatedly witness how these standards lead to what I call *emotional learning stumbling blocks* for my children. After the experience with drawing, I was concerned that my then 10-year-old son would be discouraged from pursuing other things he liked in the future if he did not assess himself as the best. About a year later, he declared that he was not going to pursue anything with math because it was "too hard" and he did not like being confused and feeling like he was "stupid." I was surprised and did not take him seriously because up to that point he had thought of himself as "good at math" and really enjoyed it, but when faced with something that he did not understand and that he kept "doing wrong" he was ready to quit. This was drawing all over again, but instead of being the best at drawing, he felt he needed to "get" math right away, and if he did not get it right away, that meant that he was not good at it.

Without any one explicitly telling him, my son had unconsciously adopted two standards for himself with respect to learning: learning had to happen fast, or else you are not smart; and if you make a mistake, your teachers and others will think that you are not smart. After some time and work, he was able to let go of those standards, thankfully, and today he is enjoying a field of study that requires quite a bit of math.

The latter standard is particularly curious: why do some people think that making a mistake will cause others to think they are not smart? We have all been inspired by and look up to people who have failed but were able eventually to succeed despite their failure, or even because of their failures. There are numerous examples, including:

- Famous authors like JK Rowling, whose first *Harry Potter* book was rejected 16 times and was told not to quit her day job. Or Dr. Seuss, beloved by many children and adults alike, (myself included, even after reading *Green Eggs and Ham* over 100 times), received 27 rejection letters when he first attempted to publish his first book, *And To Think I Saw It on Mulberry Street,* before he got a yes. Or Stephen King, whose book *Carrie* was rejected 30 times before being accepted for publishing by Doubleday.

- Successful entrepreneurs who failed with their first products, like Masaru Ibuka and Akio Morita who developed an electric rice cooker intended to become a staple in every home, but sold less than 100 units as the rice cooker either burned or undercooked the rice. Despite this failure, they kept plugging away, committed to making a business that sold electric household products, and after several other attempts, they eventually sold portable transistor radios, and SONY was born. Or Bill Gates and Paul Allen, two college dropouts who failed at a business called Traf-O-Data, but instead of giving up, they eventually created Micro-Soft, as it was originally known. Or Walt Disney, who started his first animation company in 1921 but quickly went bankrupt and allegedly ate dog food to survive. Many of us would read eating dog food as a sign that it is time to quit and try something different, but Disney did not.

- Successful athletes, like Orel Hershiser who was cut from his college baseball team his freshman and sophomore year, but went on to become one of baseball's great pitchers during the 1980s.

Reading these examples, it is easy to accept the claim that failing and making mistakes are important parts of the learning process, paving the road to eventual success. Not only should we expect to make mistakes and fail as we strive to acquire new skills and accomplish our goals, but we should also embrace these as opportunities for growth, opportunities without which we would probably plateau or stagnate in our learning.

Nevertheless, despite intellectually understanding this, many of us don't like to make mistakes or fail. We feel very uncomfortable when we do fail, or even at the thought of doing so, and we strive to avoid it at all costs, even if it means not accomplishing our goals. And, when we make them, we often ignore, conceal, or blame others for our mistakes instead. In his interesting book, *Black Box Thinking: Why Most People Never Learn From Their Mistakes*[9], Matthew Syed explores this phenomenon at length. For example, he points out that in healthcare, where mistakes are inevitably made but not systematically reported, investigated, and learned from, patients suffer premature deaths from preventable harm at an alarming rate, from 400,000 to 500,000 people per year (with one study suggesting 120,000 of these deaths being in the United States alone) if you also include facilities such as nursing homes and outpatient settings such as pharmacies. In addition, citing the Senate testimony of Joanne Disch, a clinical professor at the University of Minnesota School of Nursing, Syed points out that "the number of patients who endure serious complications is estimated to be ten times higher than the number of deaths."[10] In contrast, Syed shows that the aviation industry is set up to learn from mistakes; every plane is equipped with two black boxes, and after every accident, these are opened, data is analyzed, and the reason for the accident is sought so that changes can be made to procedure or equipment to ensure that the same mistakes are not made in future flights. Consequently, in contrast to the 400,000 to 500,000 premature deaths per year in healthcare, in 2013, 210 people died as a result of plane crashes. In 2014, partially due to the Malaysia plane crash, 641 died.

---

9 Matthew Syed, *Black Box Thinking: Why Most People Never Learn From Their Mistakes – But Some Do* (New York: Portfolio Penguin, 2016), 10 – 53.
10 Id., 10.

Syed argues that we need to redefine our relationship with failure and assume that "failure is inevitable in a complex world," which is why "learning from mistakes is so imperative." I completely agree, but how can we develop a different attitude towards mistakes and failures? Thanks to the efforts of people like Carol Dweck,[11] who promote the cultivation of a "growth mindset" so that people can, among other things, become less fearful of making mistakes, schools are becoming much more aware of the importance of teaching students that it is okay to make mistakes. However, until recently, schools have generally not been the place where we learn to make mistakes and to embrace them as an opportunity for growth.

In school, many of us acquired knowledge of certain subjects. We learned content and memorized information and formulas so that we could do well in exams. We were rewarded with good grades if we got the right answers. We were given poor marks if we got the answers wrong. In some standardized tests – like the SAT until recently, or advanced placement exams – we were penalized for guessing, so we learned to leave answers blank unless we were sure of the answer. The message was clear: learning to make mistakes is important, *but I'd better not make them!*

Unfortunately, for every child or adult who is able to work through challenges and persevere as they work to master something new, there are many of us who don't. For every Orel Hershiser there are countless kids who quit a sport they liked, and perhaps had the potential to enjoy and possibly excel in, because they failed to make the cut at some point. For every published author, there are countless others who dream about becoming a writer, but never share their writing with others. For every successful entrepreneur, there are people sitting in their cubicles not willing to embark on new ventures. We get frustrated, we feel embarrassed, and eventually, many of us conclude that *this is not worth it*, and we quit. Or, we don't even embark on a learning process because we think it may be too hard, we don't want to look stupid, we don't want others to look at us like we are a burden, or someone that does not contribute on day one. Have you tried learning another language? Those who are comfortable not understanding and making

---

11 Carol S. Dweck, *Mindset: The New Psychology of Success* (New York: Random House, 2006).

mistakes tend to learn faster; those who are not, often give up. Being from a bilingual family living in the United States, I have seen some of the younger kids struggle with Spanish and others thrive, depending on their emotional disposition towards not understanding and towards making mistakes.

We nod our heads as we read about the importance of things like cultivating a "beginner's state of mind" and "failing fast and failing often," but in real life, we often don't feel comfortable being a beginner. We don't feel comfortable not knowing. We don't feel comfortable making mistakes. We are not equipped with the basic emotional resilience to cope with the stresses and disappointments of failure. As a result, even though we understand that learning is a process that requires time and perseverance, we choose not to embark on that process, or if we do, we quit way before we reach our objectives. We get in the way of our own learning. Why does that happen and how do we stop it?

ASSESSMENTS THAT BLOCK OUR LEARNING

Why are so many of us reluctant to admit that we don't know something? Why do we get embarrassed instead of celebrating it as an opportunity to learn something new? The simple abbreviated answer is that we think we should know, or that others expect us to know. Or we think we should behave a certain way and that others expect us to behave in a certain way. Another way to describe what is going on here is that we tend to operate with certain automatic assessments. In our work, we use the notion of "assessment" as a technical term to capture the ways we operate with certain evaluative predispositions: *I like this. I don't like this. This is good. This is bad. This is the right thing to do. This is the wrong thing to do. This is appropriate. This is inappropriate.*[12] All too often, we all habitually operate with unnoticed assessments that impede our ability to learn.

---

12 Making, receiving, and exploring assessments openly, productively, and without defensiveness is pivotal for building trust and working effectively in teams. Not all of us are comfortable with our ability to do this, and it is certainly a skill that can be developed. I will say more about assessments later on when I discuss examples of people working to develop skills for making and receiving assessments. See below, 97-117. See also, Fernando Flores, *Conversations For Action and Other Essays: Instilling a Culture of Commitment in Working Relationships.* Ed. Maria Flores Letelier (CreateSpace Independent Platform, 2012). In particular, see Chapter 5, "Assertions and Assessments."

As human beings, we are constantly operating with a barrage of assessments. Often, we are not even aware that we are making these assessments, and it can be misleading to even describe them as something we actively "do" or "make," since we are often in their grip, habitually and automatically seeing and responding to things in their light. This is why we need practices to loosen the grip that our automatic assessments can have upon us, because, as I will discuss in some detail, they can easily get in the way of our learning something new.

A first step in loosening the grip that our automatic assessments can have on us is to begin to recognize them and to differentiate them from what we call "assertions." An assertion is a statement about how things are in the world. In making an assertion, I make a commitment to share observations and evidence about an established state of affairs. For example, if I assert, "It is raining," I commit myself to verifying this to you by inviting you to observe the wet sidewalk outside my window.

An assessment, on the other hand, rather than being oriented toward an already established state of affairs, is oriented toward *bringing about* (or not bringing about) a state of affairs, a change in the world. To make an assessment, then, is to be committed to acting in some way or another.

In this way, the assessments we operate with directly impact how we act and what we are prepared to do. If we assess that a dress is not suitable for us, we will not wear it. If we judge a colleague untrustworthy, we are unlikely to collaborate with him. If we think it is bad to make mistakes, we will avoid making them or we may ignore or hide them if we do. If we think it is wrong to ask for help, we will not ask for help. If we think that it is bad to not know what to do, we will avoid being in situations where we don't know something by either trying to get up to speed or simply refusing to participate.

We have the power to alter our assessments and thereby to alter our own predispositions for acting. Nevertheless, often we are not even aware of the assessments that we are making and how these impact our actions. What can be done about this?

In one of our courses, Working Effectively in Small Teams, a course which inspired this writing and which I will elaborate upon later on in the book, we developed a learning environment that places participants in situations where they don't know how to do something and hence must learn something new. As part of this environment, we use a multiplayer online role-playing game, *World of Warcraft*, which most of the participants have never played. We do not expect or require that participants have any experience playing this game. Yet, during their group exercises, when they find themselves in unfamiliar situations where we can reasonably expect them to say certain things – "I don't know how to do this" or "You seem to know how to do this, could you take over that part for now?" – those words are not uttered. Over and over again, many participants who don't know what they are supposed to do and/or how to do it do not utter such words. Instead, they usually stay quiet. They try to figure things out on their own. They make the same mistakes over and over again. They stop engaging with people on their team. Upon reflecting on their experiences after this happens to them, many report feeling frustrated, anxious, confused, and ready to give up.

As we begin to explore together what kept them from being able to say, "I don't know," so they could ask for help, they discover that they were operating with certain assessments about the situation. These assessments caused them to judge that saying "I don't know" and asking for help were not appropriate moves, moves that they "should not" make. Since they think that they "should not" ask for help and that they "should" already know this, they stay quiet, but by not speaking up and asking for help, these people realize that they thwarted their own ability to learn the new skills. In our work with hundreds of people of diverse backgrounds, I have identified five categories of assessments that get in the way of learning, assessments based on standards that they have acquired through the course of their lives that guide what they feel they should do or should know.

The list on the next page is not complete, but in my experience, these are the categories that most frequently show up as roadblocks to learning.

Common Categories of Assessments That Get in the Way of Learning

It is important to be competent.
- It is important to know the right answer.
- It is important to have the expertise required for your role.
- If you don't know what to do or how to do it, then you are incompetent.
- If you are struggling to do something, then you are incompetent.
- Being incompetent is bad.
- Making mistakes is bad. People will judge you negatively if you make mistakes.
- If you are not competent, then don't speak up. If you are not competent, stay out of the way. If you are not competent, withdraw.

It is important to be efficient.
- Learning has to happen fast.
- We must "get" things right away.
- Results have to happen quickly.
- We must not waste time.
- If we don't know something, we must get up to speed, fast.

It is important to be independent and self-reliant.
- We must not depend on others.
- If we don't know something, we need to figure it out on our own. In the meantime, stay out of the way.
- Don't be a burden. Don't ask for help.

It is important to be useful.
- We must contribute to the team right away.
- If we don't contribute, we are not useful. We will not be accepted.
- If we don't know how to do something, we can't contribute. If we can't contribute, then we are of no value to our team.
- If we are not useful, perhaps we should withdraw.

It is important to be prepared at all times.
- We must minimize or eliminate uncertainty.
- You must be in control of the situation. The more knowledge you have, the more in control you will be.
- Before you try to do something, be certain that you know exactly what you are going to do, step by step.
- If you don't know how to do it, better not do anything. If you are not absolutely certain, you might be wrong. Being wrong is bad. Making mistakes is bad.

STANDARDS BEHIND THESE ASSESSMENTS

The assessments we operate with are themselves expressions of standards we have acquired for ourselves over the course of our lives. How we came to adopt and embody the standards underlying our assessments varies from person to person. Our past experiences, our family, our culture, our professional backgrounds, have all shaped our standards for assessing the world around us. As we all undoubtedly have noticed, two people looking at the same situation may have different assessments of what is going on and reach totally different conclusions about the appropriate course of action.

Person 1: "This was a great project! Let's launch another one just like it next week!"

Person 2: "What? This project was a complete waste of time. There is no way I am ever doing it again!"

Someone trained as an engineer, for example, may negatively assess an initiative at work because it does not have clear, measurable results; yet her colleague in human resources may think the initiative was a great success because everyone seems happy and engaged.

In real life, however, standards that may be appropriate in some situations may be inappropriate in others. The standards that we have come to adopt are not necessarily wrong or bad, but in some situations, they may not serve us. Often, it becomes important to declare new standards for ourselves, particularly when we are striving to learn something new.

For example, if we adhere to the standard that we must always know the right answers – a standard that served us well as we prepared to do well in exams at school – that standard may not serve us well if we are entering a new field, undertaking a new role, or going into a new industry, where we can't possibly know what we don't know. If we strive to prepare ourselves so that we have all the information, know all the answers, and eliminate all uncertainty before we embark on a new course of action, we run the risk of never embarking at all or failing to take action. In our course, we have worked with many people who were at the top of their class in some of the best universities around the world, but when they found themselves in a situation where they did not know how to proceed, they froze up. They did not ask for help, delegate, or take action. They were embarrassed. They thought others expected them to know what to do. They thought they "should" know how to proceed. They felt paralyzed by anxiety. What if they made a mistake? What if they failed? They worried the answer was out there but they didn't have it. Sometimes they blamed others for not giving them enough information.

We have also worked with people who have gained their standards by working in hierarchical organizations, like the armed forces, where many people are very good at executing orders, but not so good at asking questions or making offers to help others. A good, competent soldier executes the orders he or she is given. This may work well up to a point, in the Army, but when placed in less hierarchical civilian situations, the soldier will most likely have to learn a new way of working with people. For example, if a former soldier who habitually operates with the assessment that asking questions is not appropriate because to be competent is to do as you are told or as you are expected to perform by your superiors, he will often feel frustrated in a civilian setting when: his performance does not meet the expectations of the person making a request of him; no one gives him an order or a request and he discovers that he is expected to make offers to his customers instead; or when he assumes that everyone has the same background of understanding, and subsequently realizes that what he thinks is important is totally different than what his colleagues think is important, and vice versa.[13]   Effective behavior in everyday civilian life is guided by a different array of standards than in the services, and accordingly, learning to ask questions, to explore actively the concerns of his colleagues or his customers, whether or not they are giving him a directive, are important skills for a soldier or former soldier to develop to successfully work with others in a civilian setting. Instead of throwing in the towel, and letting frustration derail him from successfully learning to work with civilians, this person has the opportunity to modify his standards for assessing competence in a civilian setting (both of himself and his colleagues) and hence to learn to take actions that he may have been discouraged to take in the past. He must transition from, "Do as you are told and don't ask questions" to "Ask more questions." He must shift from executing orders to making offers.

We have also worked with women who acquired standards for themselves from their work in male dominated industries. In response to often being one of the only women in their roles, many were committed to proving that they belonged at work by attempting to be unflappable and competent at all times. In light of the standard that they committed themselves to – to be competent at all times – asking for help or delegating did not show up as

_____

13 Although this example talks about a male former soldier for ease of writing, we have worked with both male and female soldiers, and this example applies to both.

possibilities for them, even when they really needed to.[14] *I am not going to be the 'weakest link.' I just have to work harder. Stay later. I'll figure it out by myself.*[15] Not surprisingly, in countless occasions, women in these industries have told us that they feel exhausted most of the time.

The standard of being competent at everything at all times is impossible to meet. We are finite. We don't have all the time in the world. We have other people or things that we are committed to, including our families. We may want to work on different things that we can't get to because we are busy showing the world that we can do everything that is on our plate. We cannot be experts at everything at all times, and we can't rapidly get up to speed on everything that we don't know and still eat and sleep. Yet, even though we understand this intellectually, when we find ourselves in a situation where we don't know what to do or how to do it, instead of asking for help, many of us become overwhelmed, and eventually want to flee, and some of us will do just that. If we want to take on more responsibilities and get a promotion at work, for example, it is important to be able to ask for help and to delegate, but in order to get more comfortable doing that, we may need to alter the standards and assessments we habitually operate with. While working hard and figuring things out by ourselves may have helped us to be an A+ student in college, it may not help us learn to be an executive who can lead multiple

---

14 The ability to delegate effectively is a skill that would benefit many of us. In a recent Gallup Study survey of 143 CEOs on the Inc. 500 list, the authors found that only one in four entrepreneurs has "high delegator talent," which they deem as essential to a business's success, especially as it grows beyond the startup phase. In other words, "75 percent of the employer entrepreneurs that Gallup studied have limited-to-low levels of Delegator talent, jeopardizing their ability to build teams that can positively influence company performance." See Sangeeta Bharadwaj Badal and Bryant Ott, "Delegating: A Huge Management Challenge for Entrepreneurs," (*Gallup Business Journal*, April 14, 2015). The ability to delegate is a skill that can be developed, and a key aspect of doing so is learning to learn so that we can be more open to learning to delegate. If we find our-selves hesitant, unwilling, or unable to delegate, we can then proceed to explore the assessments we have that keep us from learning to delegate effectively and the standards that we adhere to that may be stopping us from taking the kinds of actions that we need to learn to take. Frequent as-sessments that we have heard for not delegating include the following assessments: "It's not okay to ask for help;" "If I can do it myself, I should;" "My team does not know how to do this and it would take too much work to bring them up to speed;" "I don't trust my colleagues to do it well;" and "It's not good to depend on others; it's better to be self-reliant."
15 For an example similar to this, read the case studies in Sections 5 and 6 of this book.

projects and people at the same time. Unless we begin to adopt a new standard, we may become overwhelmed, exhausted from being under constant stress, and as a consequence, decide that taking on more responsibility is just not worth it.

Of course, discovering our standards and changing them so that we can open ourselves up to learning new skills requires more than the recognition of the need to do so. Learning is a process. It takes time. Acquiring a new skill does not happen from one second to the next. Reading about it once is not enough. We won't learn something new simply because we say we want to. A toddler does not simply say, "I want to walk" and lo and behold, begins to walk. She crawls; she learns to stand holding on to chairs, tables, or a parent's hand. Eventually, after numerous falls, collisions with furniture, and false starts, she magically takes her first step. And then she falls again, and again and again, until she masters walking. If we are to acquire a new ability, it requires personal involvement. It requires numerous iterations and recurrent practice, not throwing in the towel. Imagine our toddler giving up after falling two or three times because she felt that learning to walk was just too hard. As silly as this example seems, often this is exactly what we do, as children and as adults. We give up on doing something new as soon as we feel uncomfortable or some obstacle gets in our way, and sometimes we give up on learning something new before we even try. *I want to learn to delegate so that I have time to do everything I need to do, but I don't feel comfortable asking for help. Others will judge me negatively if I ask for help, so there is no point in me even trying to delegate.*

A critical aid to learning is opening up emotional dispositions that prompt us to take effective action. Instead of giving in to our desire to quit, we can cultivate emotional dispositions that will imbue us with the will to continue learning. I will now introduce a new dimension of the learning process that is usually overlooked: the role of *moods* in learning. The assessments that we have about any given situation often determine what we do because they shape our moods and our moods shape our tendencies to act. If we think it is inappropriate to not know something, we will likely be anxious when placed in situations where we must learn something new. If we think that it is inappropriate to ask for help, we will be reluctant to ask for the help that we require. Without us even being consciously aware of it, we fall into moods of resignation and confusion, which may lead us to give up. To successfully learn what we set out to learn, we must learn to be sensitive to the moods that we find ourselves in. These moods give us the first clue of the assessments and standards that we have that may impede our learning, and they also give us the first clue as to what actions we can take to make sure we continue to work towards achieving our learning objectives.

Our moods and our assessments are intimately linked. In particular, our moods can be decoded as involving automatic assessments of our situation as a whole, including our possibilities for intervening in the situation and changing it in some way. This link between moods and assessments gives moods their power to influence how we are predisposed to act and respond to a situation, but it is also what enables us to have influence over our own moods. If we can gain sensitivity to our moods and an ability to alter the assessments we are operating with, we can open the possibility of shifting our moods. Such a shift will then empower us to overcome the negative impact of moods that block us from learning or engaging with others. In the next section I say more about moods and how by coming to appreciate the connection of moods to assessments and standards, we can also cultivate the skills of shifting out of unproductive moods.

3

Cultivating a Predisposition to Learning: Moods

Learning to learn requires that we be in a mood that is conducive to learning. Often we are not. Working with people to help them develop new skills, we have seen over and over how many of us fall into negative moods that derail our quest for learning, or hold us back from embarking on our learning quest in the first place.

What do I mean by moods?[16] Moods are "attunements" to the situation we find ourselves in at any given moment which predispose us to certain actions. Someone who is in a blue mood will not be disposed to go to a party, while someone who is in a bored mood does not find any possibilities attractive. Someone who is in an annoyed mood will be likely to lash out at someone for trivially whistling a tune, while someone in a joyous mood might whistle along. Moods are like the coloring of how

---

16 Moods are a vast domain whose detailed exploration is well beyond the scope of this work. What I focus on in this writing, and in the work that we do during the WEST course, is but a sliver of this topic. Much of my writing in this section is based on many conversations and collaborations I have had with Fernando Flores. In a forthcoming work, he calls many of the moods that I highlight here, along with the moods that tend to show up when we work with teams, "moods of pragmatic engagement." He also identifies a broader range of moods, including, among others, the shared socio-political mood of a nation (e.g., the mood of distrust in current American politics), and the overarching mood of a whole era or epoch (e.g., the mood of uncertainty in the age of climate change). For a reader interested in diving deeper into the theme of moods, the philosopher Martin Heidegger's writings on moods and how these constitute our "being-in-the-world" may be of interest. (*Being and Time*. New York: Harper and Row, 1962). For an interesting discussion on the difference between moods and emotions, see Paul Ekman and Richard J. Davidson, *The Nature of Emotion: Fundamental Questions* (New York: Oxford UP, 1994). See also Paul Ekman, *Emotional Awareness: Overcoming the Obstacles to Psychological Balance and Compassion: A Conversation between the Dalai Lama and Paul Ekman, Ph.D.* (New York: Holt Paperback, 2008).

we encounter the world around us, what it says to us or how it appeals to us. Moods and emotions are different even though they normally come together. Emotions are directed at some particular person or some particular thing. You may be angry with your boss, and feel it in the burning of your face and the curling of your toes, because your boss did not give you the promotion she promised you. You may be sad, feeling a sinking emptiness in your stomach, because you experienced the sudden loss of a dear family member. You may be ashamed, feeling like you want to hide, because you lied and you believe that lying is wrong. Moods, although similar to emotions in that we can also sense them in our bodies, are more in the background. Most of the time, we are not even consciously aware of our moods, but they nevertheless show up in our behavior and demeanor, and the sense we have about what is possible or not possible.

In our work, we interpret moods as involving assessments that people have about their future. Sometimes we refer to them as automatic assessments, because, as mentioned above, we are usually not aware of many of the assessments that we operate with. Our history, including past experiences and culture, colors how we see the future, and predisposes us to act a certain way in the present. If we have experienced something not working in the past, we may be in a mood of resignation about that changing in the future and will be reluctant to try to take action in the present. *I have made many offers to help people on my team in the past, but no one responds to my e-mails. I guess everyone is too busy. I am not going to keep trying.* Or, *here they come again with a new change initiative. They will do a lot of stuff, but in the end nothing will change. It's always this way. I am not going to do anything to try to support what they are doing.* If we are in a mood of ambition, however, and committed to producing a result, then obstacles show up as hurdles to be overcome, not as evidence that we are never going to be successful. *I am committed to succeeding as a team, and my team member does not know what she is doing. I am going to offer to train her so that she can perform her role.* Or, *I am committed to developing a stronger relationship with our clients and I think that what we are doing will lead to that. I know that we've made mistakes in the past, but we have learned from these, and if we continue down this path, we will get there!*

We must accept our moods as facts – as human beings we are always in some mood, sometimes even multiple moods at a time – but we don't need to be hostages to them, particularly if we find that we have fallen into moods that close possibilities for us. When embarking on the process of learning something new, or even when considering embarking on the process of learning something new, we can fall into certain negative, unproductive moods that make learning much more difficult, if not impossible. We feel anxious, confused, resigned, or insecure, which makes us feel stressed and want to flee the situation. *I have no idea what to do. I'd rather quit than feel embarrassed when I fail. I'd rather give up than feel anxious all the time. It's too stressful. Who needs this?*

There is nothing wrong with us if we fall into negative moods. At some point or another, all of us do. Contrary to what many believe, we cannot *control* our moods, but if we are committed to our learning, we must learn to not allow negative, unproductive moods to get in the way of accomplishing our objectives. It is important to emphasize, however, that moods are not simply things that happen to us. They are automatic predispositions toward certain possibilities, and away from others, based on our past, and grounded in the standards of behavior we have acquired over the course of our lives. As we alluded to in the previous pages, the standards that we've acquired throughout our lives that give rise to our predispositions are not usually explicit. They operate and guide us in the background, unexamined, waiting and available to be discovered. Moods, on the other hand, are sensed.

Since moods are sensed, and since they are intimately connected with our standards for behavior and our automatic assessments of our situation, we have found that by exploring the moods we have fallen into, we can learn to shift them when necessary, and thereby open up new possibilities for action, including the possibility of declaring new standards for ourselves. This is relevant at a general level, but it is of particular importance when it comes to overcoming obstacles that may get in the way of our continued learning. The first step in developing the skill for shifting out of negative moods that block our learning is developing an ability to recognize negative or unproductive moods when they come over us.

MOODS THAT CAN BLOCK OUR LEARNING

Moods are windows to our assessments and to the standards that support them. If we become sensitive to our moods, we may be able to open the curtains and observe how we see things, and discover whether our automatic predispositions help us achieve our learning objectives or block us. The chart below reveals certain unproductive[17] moods that routinely can get in the way of learning. This is not a comprehensive list of moods that may not be conducive to learning, but I highlight those that I have observed most frequently during our work. Of course, people can also be in moods that are conducive to learning. I turn to such moods after examining the moods that block learning.

17 For the sake of this writing, I call these moods "unproductive moods." This label does not mean that these moods are inherently bad, wrong, or to be avoided at all costs. We fall into the moods that we fall into. By learning to be sensitive to them, however, we can learn not to be trapped by them if we find that they are blocking us from taking the kinds of action that we may need to take to continue to learn. The moods listed here are the moods I have often observed block people's learning. It is important to note, however, that in some situations, some of these moods may not be necessarily detrimental to our learning.

For example, a mood of impatience may or may not get in the way of learning. In some situations, it may prompt us to take action, to practice, to take risks, and to not over-analyze, which may be exactly what we need to continue to learn, particularly as we become more competent. In other situations, however, it may prompt us to disengage too quickly and not take the actions that we need to take to continue to learn. We may prematurely conclude that we are not "cut out" to do something simply because we did not give ourselves the time to learn. Similarly, the mood of skepticism may help us to take action to continue to learn, or it may block us from taking action. There is a difference between what I consider a healthy skeptical mood, where people don't blindly trust what others promise them and choose to move prudently to ensure that they are embarking on a learning process with people who are qualified to teach (e.g., check references, interview past students, etc.) and a skeptical mood that closes possibilities, where they simply refuse to believe that another person or group has something to teach them despite the evidence (e.g., results, case studies, references, degrees, etc.). If we find ourselves in a mood of skepticism, it is important to acknowledge it, and pause to explore how it is influencing our behavior. If we find, for instance, that our standard is that we should move with prudence and do our homework to make sure that the teacher we are hiring is competent, then continued learning is possible. If we find that our standard is that no one could possibly teach us anything because everyone is incompetent and not trustworthy, despite the evidence, we may want to see what we can do to begin to build trust with people who may be able to mentor us, otherwise learning may be much harder, if not impossible, for us.

Notwithstanding the helpfulness of this list for identifying the moods that we may be in, it is important to keep in mind that a mood is the window that allows us to peek in; it is up to us to do the work to discover what is inside – our automatic assessments and the standards that they are based on – and to determine whether we need to rearrange things so that they don't block us from reaching our learning objectives.

Moods that get in the way of learning

Unproductive Mood	Sample assessments that could trigger this mood
Confusion	I don't understand what is going on here, and I don't like it. Being confused is a bad thing. There is nothing of value for me here. Being confused is not good for me. I need to quickly escape this situation!
Resignation	I am too old to learn this. I am never going to be able to do this, no matter how much I try, so what's the point? This involves numbers; I was never good at math, so I am not going to be able to do this. This game requires reading a map; I am bad with maps. There is no point for me to even try this game. This is not possible.
Frustration	I tried to do this, but failed. I expected to be able to do this already. I am not getting this as fast as I think I should. This isn't working like it should.
Arrogance	There is nothing new for me to learn here. I already know all there is to know about this. Or I already know all I want to know. This is a waste of my time.
Impatience	(Often coupled with arrogance.) There is no value in what we are doing here. We need to move on. This needs to go faster. We're wasting time.
Boredom	There is nothing of value for me here. There is nothing I can do to make it less boring to me.
Fear/Anxiety[18]	I don't know how to do this. I may make mistakes. Mistakes are bad and I may not recover from them. I don't know what the right course of action is. I am going to quit, because making a mistake is worse than simply not trying.
Overwhelm	There is so much I don't know, or can't do. There is no one I can ask for help. I just have to work harder and harder, but I'll probably still fail because there isn't enough time.
Lack of Confidence (insecurity)	I am not competent to learn this. I have always been bad at math, so I am not going to be able to learn to do this since it requires math. I've never done this. I can't do this. I am not good enough to be here. Others are way smarter than I am. I am never going to get this!
Distrust or Skepticism	I don't trust that my colleague will take care of me if I tell him I don't know what to do. I think my colleague talks a good game, but I don't think she knows how to teach me what I need to know. I am not going to ask him for help as I don't think he is competent to give it to me. This process may be working for some people, but I am skeptical that it will really work for me.

---

18 By anxiety here I mean a mood of anxiety that is often reported by the people in our courses, an anxiety/fear connected to uncertainty, to not knowing what to do or to making mistakes. I am not referring to clinical anxiety or depression where a person may have lost a sense of meaning in his or her life and may not see any possibilities, impairing his or her capacity to function.

If we learn to become aware of our moods and are able to identify one or more of these moods that are not conducive to learning, we can then explore the assessments that we have about the situation, and discover the standards to which we adhere that support those assessments. This is critical to the success of the learning process. Participants in our courses regularly discover that they have fallen into moods that get in the way of achieving their learning objectives. Yet when they explore these moods, they often discover that their assessments are based on standards that are either: not relevant to the situation at hand – as with the military person not currently acting in a chain of command who must now negotiate with others to determine what actions he is going to take; or not useful for achieving their goal, as with the top college student who excelled in every topic by making sure she knew everything that would be covered on the exams, but who must now learn to make decisions while coping with uncertainty. As a result of discovering the standards to which they adhered and their inappropriateness to the current situation, participants begin to see actions that they can take to shift their unproductive moods and continue on their learning quest until they achieve their objectives.

As previously mentioned, in our courses we use an online multiplayer game as part of our learning environment. Many participants have never played this game before, or any like it. They are absolute beginners, but instead of rejoicing because they are about to learn something new, some of them quickly fall into the following moods:

Confusion: "I have no idea what to do and I don't like it!"
Impatience: "I should be getting this quicker!"
Anxiety: "I don't know what to do and if I make a mistake my team will think poorly of me."
Frustration: "I should know how to work my avatar already."
Insecurity/lack of confidence: "I have no clue what is going on here and I am never going to get it. I am bad at games. I am bad with technology. I am not going to be able to contribute to my team."

Although they can intellectually understand that they are beginners, they are not comfortable allowing themselves to *be* beginners and to undergo the learning process that goes along with it. By exploring their assessments, however, they begin to discover that they have unreasonable expectations for themselves: *I should be competent right away. I should contribute right away. By not knowing what to do, I am holding the team back.* As they discover the standards that they are holding themselves to, they realize that these standards are not helpful for learning to play the game with others. They begin to see that a beginner is not expected to contribute as an expert right way, but rather that the role of a beginner is to be a beginner: follow instructions, ask questions, and practice. If they don't follow instructions, ask questions, and practice, then they are not contributing to the team; they are not taking their role as a beginner seriously. When they realize this, their stress begins to diminish and they often begin to experience learning the game as an enjoyable process, instead of as a torturous undertaking where they have to hide their lack of skills so that others do not judge them as incompetent and undesirable members of the team.

My son, in the example about math, fell into the following moods:

Confusion: "I don't understand these math problems. I am totally confused and it is not good to not understand."
Frustration: "I should get this quickly. I am not."
Impatience: "I should understand these problems faster."
Lack of confidence: "Smart people get things fast and I am not getting this fast."
Resignation: "Since I am not getting these problems quickly, I am not good at math. I am not going to study anything that has to do with math when I get older."

In exploring these moods with him, we discovered that he had the assessment that he was not smart in math, and that he based that assessment on a standard he had already adopted for evaluating whether or not someone is smart: smart people understand things fast; if you don't understand something quickly, then you are not smart in that subject matter. Consequently, he concluded that he should not aspire to study anything that requires math when he gets older because he was no longer good in that subject. Luckily, after a number of conversations, he came to realize that this way of assessing his intelligence would not serve him well in his educational and professional career, where he will encounter, if he wants to, bigger and more difficult challenges that don't have obvious answers that people can get right away. We talked about cancer, and how many people have been trying to find a cure that is not obvious, yet how important it is for people working on a cure to persevere and not give up on trying. We talked about scientists and astrophysicists quitting their field the moment they do not get an answer right away, and what a waste that would be. My son began to see that for these people, lack of knowledge means a new frontier to explore, not something to avoid or be embarrassed by. Instead of resignation, they are in moods that are much more conducive to exploration and continued learning, such as the moods of *wonder* or *ambition*. I highlight these moods and a few others in the next section.

MOODS THAT PREDISPOSE US TO CONTINUING TO LEARN

Fortunately, just like there are moods that may limit or block our learning, there are other, opposing moods, that can predispose us to embark and stay on our learning journey. Again, this is not meant to be a comprehensive list. These are moods that we have observed repeatedly in our work and that our students strive to cultivate as they work to shift from negative moods that get in the way of their learning objectives.

Moods that are Conducive to Learning

Mood	Sample assessments that could trigger this mood
Wonder	I don't know what is going on here, but the world is full of opportunities, and I like it! Even though I don't have a clue what is going on here, I trust that there is something for me to learn, and I am excited about it. *Unlike a mood of confusion, when in a mood of wonder (or perplexity, described below) ignorance shows up as something positive, a new frontier to explore, an inspiration for our learning, not something to be embarrassed by or to be avoided.*
Perplexity	I am totally confused, but I feel it is important to explore more and possibly get answers that may be important to me. I am going to stick with this until I persevere.
Serenity/ Acceptance	I accept that the past is the past and is not in my control. I accept that the future is uncertain, it will be full of surprises, and I cannot predict it. Both good and bad will come unexpectedly, and I am grateful to life. *Unlike resignation, when we are in a mood of serenity, we accept the past as the past, but we are not resigned about our future possibilities, and we are free to take action to embrace these or walk away from these.*
Patience	I accept that learning requires that I practice recurrently over a period of time. That is the way learning works.
Ambition	I see opportunities here. I may not be fully prepared and I am not certain of everything that may come my way, but I am convinced that my full commitment to this is valuable. I am committed to take action. *When we are in a mood of ambition, setbacks show up as challenges to navigate and master, not as evidence that what we set out to accomplish is not possible, as they might be interpreted by someone who is in moods of resignation, insecurity, or anxiety, for example.*
Resolution	I see opportunities here and I am going to take action right now.
Confidence	I have successful experience in this area, and I am competent to act in this situation. I have been able to learn new things before, and I am going to be able to do it again. I have people that I can ask for help, who will take care of me. *When in a mood of confidence, lack of competence shows up as something to master, not as a reason to give up.*
Trust	I am learning from people who have experience in the area I want to learn from. They have produced results. They have a good reputation. I can learn from them. They care about supporting my learning. They are not going to judge me negatively if I don't know something.

Learning to shift from unproductive to productive moods is a critical aspect of learning to learn. As we learn to become aware of our moods, and are able to observe ourselves in a negative mood that blocks us from achieving what we want to achieve, such as resignation, we can choose not to remain hostages to this mood, and take action to cultivate an alternative mood that is more conducive to achieving what we set out to achieve.

SHIFTING FROM UNPRODUCTIVE MOODS TO MOODS THAT ARE CONDUCIVE TO LEARNING

As you might expect, the first step to developing the ability to shift your mood is to become aware of your mood(s). This is a skill that takes practice, but with practice it can be learned, and the more you practice, the easier it becomes. When we first introduce the distinctions of moods to participants in our courses, some are a bit perplexed and the conversation may seem a bit awkward to them, but as the weeks go by, they become much more aware of their own moods, and the moods of their colleagues.

Meditative practices and mindfulness can be very useful in helping us to develop the ability to be present to the moods we find ourselves in, but when engaged in the process of learning something new, it is essential that we not stop at simply observing the moods and emotions that we find ourselves in, but that we do so for the purpose of seeing what action we may need to take to make it possible for us to continue to learn and eventually achieve our objectives. This is not necessarily inconsistent with a practice of mindfulness. As B. Allan Wallace argues, mindfulness also includes "*retrospective* memory of things in the past, *prospectively* remembering to do something in the future, and present centered recollection in the sense of maintaining unwavering attention to a present reality."[19] Nevertheless, I think it is important to emphasize the importance of combining learning to be aware of our moods with a wider practice of reflection aimed at helping us to successfully navigate the learning process.

---

19 Ekman, Emotional Awareness: Overcoming the Obstacles to Psychological Balance and Compassion, 56 – 57.

In our work, although we have not included meditative practices, we do focus on cultivating an awareness of our moods in a given situation for the sake of discovering what mental habits, or predispositions, we may need to abandon, modify or cultivate, and for coming to a resolution on action we may want to take to accomplish what we want to accomplish in the future, including learning a new skill. We have found that asking people to reflect on their moods, either when they are immersed in an activity or immediately afterwards, begins to focus them on observing how they observe what is going on around them. Among other things, they become aware of the following: their bodily sensations, such as increased heart rate, stomach tightness, or increased blood flow to their hands; their assessments of the situation and the underlying standards upon which they base them; what they think should or should not be happening; and what they see as possible or not possible. With our guidance at first, they ask themselves questions that help them to identify and explore their mood and their past experiences that may have molded it, they are then encouraged to evaluate whether their automatic interpretations are appropriate for the situation at hand or whether they block their learning and what they would like to achieve. If the latter, then participants can explore what action they can begin to take to modify these and to cultivate alternative moods that are more conducive to their continued learning.

If we become aware that we have fallen into an unproductive mood, sometimes we can cultivate more productive moods simply by doing exercise or listening to music. We can go for a run to clear our head. Or, we can watch a beautiful movie and get inspired by new possibilities. A college professor once told me that she adopted the practice of auditing graduate seminars whenever she began to feel that it was not possible to do anything new given the bureaucratic demands of her institution. She said, "It's contagious to be around people who are excited and ambitious about what they are doing!" But if these things are not enough, and usually they are not if we have a deeply embedded predisposition regarding what we can or cannot do, we can learn to shift our mood(s).

If you become aware that you have fallen into an unproductive mood, the following process of reflection and action can enable you to take action to shift this mood and not allow it to block your learning:

1. *Reflect on your learning objective.* Reflect on the future that you are committed to bringing about. In other words, why do you care to develop this skill in the first place? For the sake of what is this skill important to me? If you don't abandon your learning process, what would you be able to do that you can't do now?

For example, if I want to develop my delegation skills, why would this be of benefit to me? Perhaps I want to be able to take on more responsibility at work so that I can be promoted. Or perhaps I am working 24/7 and would like to be able to do other things. If this is important to me, then does it make sense to keep the status quo and give up on learning to delegate effectively? Or, if I have a top-down style of leadership, why is it important for me to learn to work in a more inclusive style of leadership? Do I need my team to be stronger and more independent of me so that I don't have to be involved in every detail and perhaps can begin to focus on other things that I care about? Or do we need to produce bigger results than we are producing, or that I can produce by myself even if I work non-stop?

Articulating why developing this skill is important and of benefit to you and/or others can enable the emergence of a mood of ambition that will motivate you to continue learning, despite the challenges that you face. Unproductive moods are part of the process, obstacles that you will likely encounter along the way, but not allowing yourself to be trapped by them is crucial to reaching the learning objectives that are important for you.

2. *Identify and explore the unproductive mood.* Is the mood similar to one of the ones identified earlier in this book? Reflect on past experiences that may trigger the mood that is not conducive to you achieving your learning objectives. What are the assessments that you have about yourself in this learning situation? What are the standards giving

rise to those assessments? Are these relevant to the situation that you find yourself in? Do they help you reach your objectives or do they hinder you?

For example, if you discover that you are in moods of resignation and impatience about learning to build a strong team in order to focus on things that you are not able to focus on today, you may find that you have the following types of assessments:

- *My team is incompetent.*
- *My team can never learn to become competent.*
- *No matter what I ask of them, my team is always going to do a poor job and I am going to have to do the work myself.*
- *There is no point to delegate anything to members of my team because whatever I delegate will simply come back to me, and I will have to do it.*
- *It's best if I do things by myself instead of wasting time making requests of my team.*

Are these assessments well grounded?[20] What are the standards that you are using for assessing the team's competence? Do you expect everyone to be ready to fully contribute on day one? Is there a learning curve or should you expect people that report to you to be just as competent as you? Should they know their roles and your expectations without you talking with them about it? Are they new to the company? To the industry? To your team? Are there some things that they can be trusted to do? And are there some things that are important for them to learn so that they can perform more effectively in the future? Is there really nothing that can be done to increase your team's competence? As you explore these questions, you may find that your assessments are not helpful to reaching your objective, and that there are, in fact, actions that you can take now to begin to build a strong team.

---

20 For more on assessments, including what it takes to ground them effectively, see section 5 of this book.

3. *Identify moods that would be more conducive to reaching your learning objectives.* What are the assessments that are connected to these moods?

For example, if you are in a mood of resignation, a mood of ambition and resolution may make it possible for you to continue to work towards reaching your objectives. If you are in a mood of insecurity, developing confidence could be important. If you are in a mood of distrust, what could you do to cultivate trust?

4. *Speculate what action you could take to shift the unproductive moods to moods that will be more conducive to your learning objectives.*

In the example in number 2 above, if you identified that you have fallen into moods of resignation and impatience, what can you do to begin to cultivate a mood of ambition and resolution instead? *I see opportunities here. My full commitment to this is valuable. I am committed to take action.* These are the kinds of assessments behind moods of ambition and resolution. What are the opportunities here for you? If your team becomes more competent, what will they be able to do that they can't do now? What would you be able to do if you were able to delegate more responsibility to them? What can you do to begin to shift out of a mood of impatience? *I accept that learning is a process and it requires time and perseverance. I can take action to create the future I want to create.* These are assessments that could help you cultivate a mood of serenity and patience about the process, moods that will help you stick to your learning process rather than abandon it at the first hurdle. What can you trust your team to do? What is missing? What can you do to help them develop further so that they can incrementally take on more responsibility? By reflecting on these moods, and exploring possible actions to take that will enable you to successfully grow your team, you will likely become more resolved to not give up on your learning objective, and to take action to help you achieve it instead. As a result, you can resolve to take different types of action, such as: request someone to help you train your team; declare the practice of meeting with your team members on a regular basis so that you can orient them more to your business and to the challenges the company or your team has to meet; and/or continue to practice delegation, but commit to giving people feedback right away so that they can take corrective action and/or learn to do it better next time.

5. *Take action.* Learning a new skill requires that you take action. You are very unlikely to learn to do something new without actually trying to do it and engaging in continued practice over a prolonged period of time. Since the early 1990s, advances in neuroscience have demonstrated the plasticity of the brain, the notion that the brain is "neither immutable nor static, but continuously remodeled by the lives we live."[21] In other words, the human brain is not fixed after childhood; it is malleable, flexible and it can continuously learn to adapt to new situations throughout our lives. By engaging in a practice of reflection and action, you are not only evaluating how you are doing and making adjustments to your behavior accordingly, you are also making new connections in your brain and, to borrow the word of Dr. Richard Davidson, "remodeling" it.[22] And, like any remodel, it requires action and some time. Further, learning a new skill often requires unlearning deeply embedded interpretations that show up as automatic emotional dispositions and habits that may make you want to quit. Giving yourself the gift of patience and the gift of time is essential.

By committing ourselves to a learning objective, we embark on a roller coaster ride of moods, some of which are conducive to reaching our learning objectives and some of which may derail us if we don't pay attention. This is an inevitable part of the learning process, but fortunately, it is something that we can learn to successfully manage by taking steps such as the ones I have

---

21 Richard J. Davidson and Sharon Begley, *The Emotional Life of Your Brain: How Its Unique Patterns Affect the Way You Think, Feel and Live – and How You Can Change Them*, (New York: Plume Publishers, 2012), 172. For another fascinating book on brain plasticity, see Norman Doidge, *The Brain that Changes Itself: Stories of Personal Triumph from the Frontiers of Brain Science* (Penguin Books, 2007).
22 Davidson and Begley, *The Emotional Life of Your Brain*, 172.

outlined here whenever we find ourselves in unproductive moods that may block us from advancing towards our learning objectives.[23]

---

23 To this end, I believe that efforts to bring to the classroom new practices inspired by Professor Carol Dweck's book, *Mindset: The New Psychology of Success, such as Mary Cay Ricci's Mindsets in the Classroom: Building a Culture of Success and Student Achievement in Schools* (Prufrock Press, 2013), are helpful and an important start in educating children about the fundamental role moods play in the learning process. While Professor Dweck focuses on "mindset," I prefer to focus on "moods," although there is clearly an overlap. Nevertheless, I think it is important to differentiate between the two as I am confident that we can go further in helping children (and adults) develop the ability to successfully navigate the shifting moods they experience and accomplish what they want to accomplish in the classroom and beyond for the rest of their lives.

By reminding us about the plasticity of the brain and the connections that get made when struggle and eventual learning take place, Professor Dweck argues that we can cultivate a *growth mindset*, which will in turn lead us to become more perseverant, resilient, less fearful of making mistakes, and more capable of committing to the effort required to achieve what we want to achieve. While I agree that taking action to cultivate moods that are conducive to learning, like self-confidence and perseverance, is very important to accomplishing our learning objectives, it is also important to acknowledge that *all of us* – even those who are committed to being open to learning and to cultivating a *growth mindset* – will fall into negative unproductive moods from time to time, and if we don't pause to explore them and resolve to shift them, these can end up limiting our learning.

Moods are not fixed things that happen in an individual's mind. We fall into them as a result of the way we engage with and interpret the world around us. Hence, aspiring to a growth mindset can be helpful, but the end objective is not whether you judge yourself to have a fixed mindset or a growth mindset, but whether you can learn to cultivate moods that will enable you to be more open to learning and to accomplish what you want to accomplish, which, I am sure, is Professor Dweck's objective too. As I state earlier in this book, human beings are always in a mood, multiple ones at once, which color what we see as possible or not. The mood we may find ourself in is triggered by predispositions that we have that are based on our past life experiences and the values or standards that we have come to adopt, consciously or unconsciously. No matter what, we will find ourselves experiencing a roller coaster of moods on a regular basis, and learning to identify, explore, and shift these when they block our learning is an important part of the learning process, and it is something that we can, with practice, certainly learn to do.

4

Navigating Each Stage of the Learning Process

I f we succeed in overcoming the obstacles that deter us from allowing ourselves to learn something new, then we can be on our way. Simply embarking on the process of learning, however, does not guarantee success. There will be breakthroughs and breakdowns along the way, and although these are important for our learning, we need to be aware that often accompanying the inevitable breakdowns there will be negative moods that may preclude our learning, unless we learn to identify and navigate them. In this section, I discuss the various stages of the typical learning process, and the common moods that tend to arise at each stage. By familiarizing ourselves with these, we will be better equipped to be on the lookout for negative moods and to take action when we find that we have fallen into moods that are not conducive to our learning.

DREYFUS' SKILL ACQUISITION MODEL

In a very useful paper for reflecting on what happens when we embark on a learning process, Hubert and Stuart Dreyfus present a model for the acquisition of skills.[24] They propose six stages of learning: beginner, advanced beginner, competent, proficient, expert, and master. They argue that depending on the stage of learning that we find ourselves in, we can expect to

---

24 Stuart E. Dreyfus and Hubert L. Dreyfus, *A Five-Stage Model of the Mental Activities Involved in Direct Skill Acquisition*. (U of California, Berkeley Operations Research Center, 1980).

experience different sorts of performance breakthroughs, challenges, and emotions. For example:

- A beginner follows instructions and explicit rules from teachers and/or manuals, assuming he or she is not simply proceeding by trial and error. S/he does not feel accountable for results, or at least should not feel accountable for results, although as we have seen with our students, they often have unreasonable expectations of themselves at this stage, and feel anxious and stressed if they think they are not fully contributing right away. A beginner may feel "uncomfortable, unsettled, anxious, but is willing to tolerate these for the sake of learning."
- A competent person is familiar with the rules and can execute the standard practices of a domain. The number of potentially relevant elements and procedures that the learner is able to recognize and follow is much greater than those she had to manage at earlier stages of learning, and can become overwhelming. To cope with this overload, a competent person adopts a plan or a perspective; she seeks rules and reasoning procedures to decide what to do. Coping can be frightening and exhausting at this stage.

The Dreyfus brothers argue that for someone to successfully acquire new skills, they must be emotionally engaged, and must be willing to take risks and make mistakes. "For embodied emotional beings like us, success and failure do matter."[25] Describing the work of Patricia Brenner with nurses at each stage of skill acquisition, Hubert Dreyfus says that unless a trainee stays "emotionally involved and accepts the joy of a job well done, as well as the remorse of mistakes, he or she will not develop further, and will eventually burn out trying to keep track of all the features and aspects, rules and maxims required. Resistance to involvement and risks leads to stagnation and ultimately boredom and regression."[26]

---

25 Hubert L. Dreyfus, *On the Internet* (London: Routledge, 2001), 37.
26 Id., 38.

I agree, but in our experience the requirement that we be emotionally engaged so that we can continue to develop our skills can be detrimentally taxing if we don't learn to accept and navigate this as part of the learning process. Learning to navigate our emotional engagement is an essential part of learning to continue to learn throughout the various stages of learning. Just as there are unproductive moods that keep us from embarking on the learning process in the first place, there are unproductive moods that may show up after we have embarked that will not let us achieve our learning goals. A person who believes that it is important to always have the right answer will find it very stressful to be in a situation where she does not know the right answer, and where she may possibly make the wrong plan and fail, if she feels accountable to others for the results. Even though she has reached a skill level of "competent," it may, as the Dreyfus brothers suggest in their paper, become too frightening and exhausting to continuously have to decide what to do, how to do it, and to risk being wrong, and as a consequence, she may quit before reaching a higher stage of mastery.

Table 1, based on the Dreyfus model[27], elaborates on their definition of each stage of learning and what we can expect a learner to be able to do at each stage.

Table 1: Dreyfus' Stages of learning

Stage of Learning	Definition	Behavior Guidelines
Beginner	A beginner has declared that s/he is going to learn to do something. S/he follows instructions and rules (general requests). Does not recognize contexts. Here a person does not need to think; s/he just does what s/he is told to do.	Student follows rules and procedures.
Advanced Beginner	Similar to a beginner, but at this stage, a person begins to recognize different situations. I.e., different rules for different situations. Advanced beginner tends to be more task-oriented.	Student has limited experience and can perform basic tasks. Advanced beginner does not yet have much involvement.
Competent	A competent person has more experience and can execute the standard practices of the domain s/he is learning. Potentially relevant elements and procedures that a learner is able to recognize are much greater. At this state, a person begins to be more goal-oriented and to feel responsible for choices.	With more experience, a competent person begins to figure out patterns and principles. Rules become rules of thumbs or guidelines. To cope, s/he learns to devise plans or choose a perspective; develops/adopts rules of thumbs or guidelines.
Proficient	A proficient person has a lot more experience, and generally sees what needs to be done, but may not yet know how to do it. Instinct and intuitions begin to kick in, but the person still needs to decide what to do or how to do it.	Rules replaced by situational discrimination. S/he sees goals and salient aspects, but not necessarily what to do to achieve those goals. To decide what to do, s/he will fall back on rules and maxims.
Expert	The expert not only sees what needs to be done, but given his/her vast repertoire of situational discriminations, s/he immediately sees how to achieve this goal.	An expert functions almost entirely by intuition and hardly at all on analysis and comparison of alternatives.
Master	A master is an expert who can generate new discourses and disciplines from anomalies in the domain. A master is dedicated to excellence in his/her profession and is not satisfied with what is accepted as "expert behavior."[28]	A master reinvents rules; generates new discourses and disciplines from anomalies in the domain. A master is willing to override the perspective that s/he intuitively experiences and chooses a new one for the sake of learning and contributing to his/her field. A master is willing to regress to earlier stages in the learning scale for the sake of taking risks and learning.

---

27 Dreyfus, *On the Internet*, pages 31 – 46.
28 Stuart E. Dreyfus and Hubert L. Dreyfus, *Beyond Expertise: Some Preliminary Thoughts on Mastery*. Published in *A Qualitative Stance*. Ed. Klaus Nielsen (Aarhus UP, 2008), 113-124.

At each of the stages of learning, not only are we able to accomplish different things, but we are also subject to fall into different moods. Below is a brief discussion of our observations on the emotional dispositions that tend to show up regularly at each of these stages, along with some guidelines on what actions we can take to stay committed to our learning process, continue to advance, and eventually reach our objectives.

EMOTIONAL DISPOSITIONS AT EACH STAGE AND GUIDELINES FOR ADVANCING TO NEXT LEVEL

Beginner

"I want to learn something new and I am committed to doing so. I am just starting out and I don't know what to do."

A beginner may feel uncomfortable in his or her novice role, but is willing to tolerate discomfort for the sake of learning. People who are not willing to tolerate this discomfort will find it quite difficult if not impossible to be a beginner, or to even embark in the learning process.[29]

A mood that is not conducive to learning at this stage, among others, is confusion. In confusion, a person sees that s/he does not know something, and doesn't like it. S/he has the assessment that it is bad not to know something. S/he wants to avoid those situations and may start to entertain the idea of giving up and doing so if she is unable to persevere. Moods that are more conducive to learning include the moods of perplexity and wonder. In these moods, a person knows that she doesn't know something, but is resolved and ambitious to figure it out.

Also, a mood of impatience and unfounded high expectations about how fast a person should be able to do something can lead to frustration for a beginner as well. A mood of insecurity can also be present in the background

---

29 For an example of someone who found himself in this situation, see Robert's case study later in the book.

as the person may expect that they "should get" things quickly, and if they don't, they may make the assessment that this is too hard for them, or that they are not smart enough for it. The beginner may fall into resignation about the possibility of learning if s/he makes a few mistakes or fails once or twice. If a beginner finds himself or herself in any of these moods, or a combination of them, or possibly all of them, which is very possible, it will be important for him or her to look at what moods they may need to cultivate instead so that s/he can shift out of the moods that will not let him or her achieve his or her learning objectives.

Besides perplexity and wonder to oppose the mood of confusion, a beginner will benefit from cultivating a mood of confidence in her ability to learn, and a mood of trust in the learning process, including her teachers and mentors. The moods of patience, serenity, and resolution are helpful at this stage as well: learning is a process that takes time. Our nervous system requires time. If we don't give ourselves time, we will not learn. We may not know what to do or how to do it, we will make mistakes, we will fail, but if we practice, learn from our mistakes, and give ourselves time to learn, we will be fine.

To continue learning, a person must gain more experience by continuing to practice. To continue to improve, it is important for a beginner to cultivate a mood of confidence in his or her ability to learn and to seek out teachers/mentors that can guide him or her and give him or her feedback, including how well s/he is doing following the rules. If a beginner falls into moods that are not conducive to learning at this stage, such as confusion, resignation, insecurity, frustration and impatience, it is important for the beginner to pause and reflect on those moods as recommended in the previous section of this book. To recap:

- Reflect on your learning objective. Why do you want to learn this skill? What would you be able to accomplish if you develop it? What would you be able to do that you are not able to do now?

- Identify and explore your unproductive mood. What are the assessments that are giving rise to your mood? What are the standards underlying these assessments? Are these standards relevant to your situation? Do they need to be modified?
- Identify moods that would be more conducive to reaching your objectives. If you are in a mood of confusion, a mood of perplexity or wonder may be more useful to you. If you are in a mood of insecurity, building a mood of confidence could be important.
- Speculate what action you could take to shift the unproductive moods to moods that would be more conducive to reaching your objectives. For example, if you are in a mood of insecurity about your ability to learn, what action can you take to cultivate a mood of confidence? Can you ask someone to be a mentor to you? Can you ask people to practice with you? How have you successfully learned in the past? Could that be useful to you here?
- Take action. Ask someone to mentor you. Request others to help you and to practice with you. To navigate your mood successfully, you must act.

During this reflection process, conversations with mentors and teachers can be extremely helpful in aiding a beginner to navigate his/her moods, particularly if the beginner does not have much mastery in doing so yet.

Advanced Beginner

"I have been practicing for a bit and generally know how to do the basic moves. I am pretty comfortable, but maybe I am becoming too comfortable."

Similar to a beginner, an advanced beginner is still following instructions and learning rules, but s/he feels more comfortable and at ease performing basic elements of a new skill. An advanced beginner is more confident in his or her abilities to perform basic moves, but can become disengaged if s/he stops being challenged.

Boredom may show up as an impediment to learning at this state. Unless an advanced beginner challenges him or herself, s/he may get stuck here and eventually get bored. S/he may feel that something is easy, perhaps too easy, and unless s/he has a compelling reason for continuing to practice and take risks that take him or her beyond his or her comfort zone for the sake of continuing to learn, the advanced beginner may not progress much further and his or her initial learning objectives may not be accomplished.

To continue to develop, it is important the advanced beginner cares about what s/he is doing. Conversations that can help to cultivate a mood of ambition about learning objectives are important to motivate advanced beginners to continue to practice, and to take risks that are outside of their comfort zone. In addition, cultivating a mood of confidence in ability to learn and trust in the process of learning is important as well. It's okay to do things outside of your comfort zone. This is the only way to continue to grow.

If you are at the advanced beginner stage of learning and find yourself in a mood that is not productive to your efforts to learn, such as boredom, it is important to take a pause, and engage in the reflection process recommended in the previous section. I will not list each question again, but at this stage it is worth emphasizing that if you are to continue to develop, it is crucial to become more engaged. To inspire you with a desire to engage, what actions could you take to cultivate a mood of ambition? What could you commit to do if you continue to develop your skills? What actions can you take to be more involved? What could you do to push yourself out of your comfort zone for the sake of accomplishing your learning objectives and not quitting along the way?

Competent
"I feel responsible for producing results, but I don't always know what to do or how to do it. It's a bit overwhelming."

As a person acquires more experience, s/he starts to feel accountable. At this stage of learning, results depend on the perspective or plan adopted by the learner. There is more uncertainty and risk. Coping can become frightening and exhausting.

As a person becomes more accountable, it is not uncommon for him or her to fall into a mood of anxiety. Since it is up to him or her to choose what to do, and his or her decision may be wrong, he or she may fear making mistakes and failing. A mood of overwhelm may show up at this stage as well. The competent person may feel that there is so much that s/he does not know how to do, and there is nothing she can do about it, except work really hard and still fail. A mood of frustration and a mood of resignation can also show up for competent performers as they may feel that there is nothing they can do to be on top of everything they expect themselves to be responsible for.

At this stage, we have found that a mood of confidence in their ability to learn, including their ability to ask for help, is very important to continue learning. A mood of trust in the learning process and in their teachers, mentors, colleagues and/or fellow students can have a significant impact in the continued learning of people who have reached this stage of learning. If they know they can ask for help and that others will help them, not knowing, taking risks, and making mistakes seem a lot less scary.

To advance to the next level, the Dreyfus brothers state that a person must experience emotions associated with success and failure. Positive emotional experiences will strengthen successful responses, and negative emotional experiences will inhibit unsuccessful responses. If a competent performer finds him or herself in moods of overwhelm, anxiety, resignation, insecurity, and distrust, it is important for the person to take action to cultivate opposite, more productive moods such as confidence, serenity, ambition, and resolution. To do so, we recommend, once again, that s/he pause and engage in the reflection process outline in section 3.

As you engage in this reflection process, you may identify that you are in a mood of anxiety and discover that you adhere to the standard that one can never make mistakes. Does this standard help or hinder you in reaching your learning goals? In a world where we can't possibly know everything that we don't know, don't mistakes provide us with a wealth of knowledge about what to do or not do in the future? Should you adopt another standard? Moods of confidence and serenity could help you continue to learn. We don't set out to make mistakes and to fail when we are trying to learn something new, but making mistakes and failing are an important and required part of the learning process. We can recover from them and learn from these, which is what will allow us to continue to learn and to grow. What action could you take to cultivate these moods? Can you engage the support of mentors or colleagues? Can you take small steps and get feedback as to how well you do? If you are an executive trying to figure out what to do next, can you declare pilot projects that would allow you to learn what works, what does not work, and recover from the latter? Declare new action and take it.

Proficient

"I generally know what needs to get done, but I don't always know how to do it. It can get a bit frustrating at times."

A proficient person is confident in his or her ability to know what needs to be done. Action becomes easier and less stressful as a person at this stage of learning generally sees what to do,[30] but since s/he does not always intuitively know how to do what s/he sees needs to be done, s/he may fall into moods of frustration and impatience if s/he expects to be able to do what s/he sees need to be done, but cannot yet do it. This could eventually lead to other unproductive moods, including resignation: "I know what I need to do, but for some reason, I can't do it! This is too much stress. Perhaps it's time to quit."

---

30 Dreyfus, *On the Internet*, 40.

If a person at this level finds him or herself in a mood of frustration and impatience, s/he will need to shift out of them so as to not allow them to derail him or her from reaching his/her objectives. Again, pausing and engaging in the aforementioned reflection process to see what actions s/he needs to take will be beneficial to the person's continued learning. We have found that often people find themselves in moods of frustration and of impatience (which often show up at the same time) because they have unrealistic expectations about what they should be able to do. They think that they should know how to do something faster than they are actually able to do it. In our courses, for example, once people begin to see what they need to do to build trust, they sometimes get frustrated because they don't immediately produce the result they want. However, at this stage, they may see what needs to be done, and they may see how they can do it, but they still need more experience and practice over a prolonged period of time until they embody this skill and can consistently produce the results they want to produce.

Accordingly, to continue to advance, a proficient person needs more experience before s/he can react automatically. Caring is important. S/he must work on things that matter to him or her so that s/he is motivated to accomplish what needs to be done. A detached case study method is not enough if the person is to continue to practice and to continue to learn from variations about what s/he is doing in order to continue to improve. Cultivating moods of ambition and resolution to get the proficient person to advance to the next level is important. What actions could a person take to cultivate ambition and resolution? If you are at this stage of learning, you will be well served to seek out mentors and colleagues that can help you navigate your moods so that you can accomplish what you set out to accomplish.

Expert

"I generally know what needs to get done and how to do it. Listen to me. Sometimes, I may not listen to others because I already know what to do."

An expert is confident in his/her ability to produce positive results. At this stage, a person depends almost entirely on intuition.[31] An expert is goal-oriented, and thanks to his or her vast repertoire of situational discriminations, is at ease with making subtle changes and adopting different approaches to reach a goal.

An expert is at ease with uncertainty in her domain of expertise, but may, at times, fall into a mood of arrogance that prevents him/her from listening to others and from fully exploring what may be going on. What is obvious to the expert may not be so obvious given new situations s/he may find him or herself in. A mood of arrogance may show up as an obstacle to learning at this stage as the person may not be predisposed to listening or to asking questions and exploring: "I already know all there is to know" about how to do this. We jokingly refer to this mood as "expertitis" – a "disease" common to experts which may stagnate continued growth and prevent an expert from reaching a "master" level if s/he so desires. Experts can be quick to find the right answer or solutions, but they may not be open to exploring others' assessments and proposed alternatives.

Also, experts in one domain of expertise often expect themselves to be experts in other domains, and when they find themselves in situations where they may not know how to do something, they may feel very uncomfortable and vulnerable. "I get paid for my expertise," an expert told me once. "If I don't know what to do, then I don't belong on this team." If an expert has the assessments that s/he must know everything, that it is bad for her/him not to know, and that others will think less of him or her if s/he doesn't know what to do, s/he is less likely to allow him or herself to return to a lower level of learning and hence be open to learn something new again. The moods of confusion, frustration, insecurity, and distrust will engulf him/her, and will make continued learning unlikely. As such, if an expert finds him or herself in one or more of those moods, it is important

---

31 Id., 42

for him/her to pause and engage in the reflection process outlined before so that s/he can take action to enable him or herself to continue learning, if he or she wants to do so.

To advance to the next level, an expert must be willing to override the perspective that as an expert performer s/he intuitively experiences. In other words, s/he forsakes the available appropriate performance and risks regression in performance for the sake of trying a new approach.[32] S/he is willing to go back to being a beginner or competent learner, for example, for the sake of exploring paths that are not obvious to him/her. S/he is open to the idea that there is more for him or her to learn, and doesn't have the assessment that it is bad for him or her to not know everything. Moods of confidence in his or her ability to learn and trust in the learning process and others are important to enable the expert to take risks. It is important to practice suspending judgment and cultivating moods of wonder and exploration to combat a mood of arrogance that may show up from time to time. Mastery requires motivation, and an expert seeking to achieve it must cultivate moods of ambition and resolution.

Master

"I am able to perform intuitively in this domain of expertise, but I'm committed to do more. I see possibilities for continued innovation and/or for making new contribution to my field."

Only a small fraction of domain experts reach mastery,[33] and in our work, we have not had much experience working with people as they endeavored to reach this stage. However, I speculate that the cultivation of moods that are conducive to continuing to learn beyond the expert level is crucial to motivating those who have reached the master level to continue learning. I speculate that the moods of ambition, resolution, wonder, and perplexity are key to people not only reaching mastery, but also

---

32 Id., 42.
33 Dreyfus and Dreyfus, *Beyond Expertise*, 113 – 124.

continuing to be motivated to learn, to risk regression in performance, to pursue anomalies, and to disregard what may come intuitively to them for the sake of innovating or contributing to their field. Similarly, I speculate that a master may stop learning, and perhaps regress to expert level, if s/he falls into moods that are not conducive to continued learning such as arrogance and resignation as these moods will cause the master to be less inclined to look for anomalies or to do anything other than what already comes intuitively to him or her.

For a summary of the emotional dispositions that tend to show up at each stage, both productive and unproductive ones, and some guidelines for continuing to learn and advancing to the next stage, see Table 2. For a quick reference of the moods that we tend to fall into at each stage, see Figure 1.

For extended case studies showing how one can learn to learn by learning to navigate one's predisposition to learning, please see the next section.

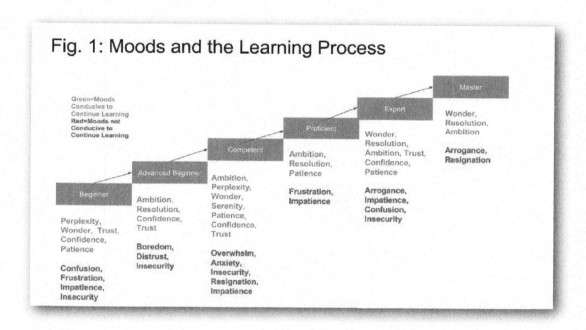

Fig. 1: Moods and the Learning Process

Table 2: Summary of Emotional Dispositions in Stages of Learning and Guidelines to Advancing to Next Level

Stage of Learning[34]	Emotional Dispositions	Guidelines to Advancing to Next Level
Beginner	A beginner may feel uncomfortable in his or her novice role but is willing to tolerate discomfort for the sake of learning. *Moods not conducive to learning:* Confusion, impatience, frustration, insecurity *Moods conducive to learning:* Perplexity, wonder, confidence, trust, patience.	A person must gain more experience by continuing to practice. To continue to improve, it is important for a beginner to cultivate moods that help him or her endure the discomfort s/he may be experiencing so that s/he continues to practice. Confidence in his/her ability to learn and trust in the learning process is important. If a beginner falls into moods that are not conducive to continuing to learn, it is important for a beginner to engage in a process of reflection outlined in section 3 of this book. Conversations with mentors/teachers about this can be very helpful as a beginner learns to navigate his/her moods.
Advanced Beginner	An advanced beginner is still following instructions and learning rules, but s/he feels more comfortable and at ease performing basic elements of a new skill. S/he can become disengaged if s/he stops being challenged. *Moods not conducive to learning:* Boredom. *Moods Conducive to learning:* Confidence, ambition, and resolution.	To advance to the next level, an advanced beginner must become more involved. S/he must care about what s/he is doing. S/he must take more risks. Cultivating a mood of ambition is important to motivate more engagement and risk-taking. Confidence in ability to learn and trust in learning process is important for an advanced beginner to be willing to take risks. If an advanced beginner finds herself bored, again it is important to engage in the process outlined in section 3.
Competent	At this stage a person feels more accountable. Results depend on the perspective or plan adopted by the learner. And since a learner will encounter many different types of situations, many of which s/he cannot possibly be fully prepared for, there is more uncertainty and risk. Coping can become frightening and exhausting. Fear of failure or fear of making mistakes is not uncommon. *Moods not conducive to learning:* Overwhelm, anxiety, resignation, frustration. *Moods conducive to learning:* Ambition, confidence, serenity and trust in others and in the learning process.	To advance to the next level, the Dreyfus brothers state that a person must experience emotions associated with success and failure. Positive emotional experiences will strengthen successful responses, and negative emotional experiences will inhibit unsuccessful responses. Cultivation of the moods of ambition and resolution is important at this stage so that these negative experiences show up as hurdles to be overcome as part of the process, and not as reasons for quitting. If a person at this stage finds him or herself in unproductive moods, it is important for him or her to engage in the reflection process outlined in section 3.

34. Dreyfus, On the Internet, pages 31 – 46.

Stage of Learning	Emotional Dispositions	Guidelines to Advancing to Next Level
Proficient	A proficient person is confident in his or her ability to know what needs to be done. Action becomes easier and less stressful as person generally sees what to do,[35] but s/he does not always intuitively know how to do what s/he sees needs to be done. *Moods not conducive learning*: Frustration, impatience, and resignation. *Moods conducive to learning*: Ambition, resolution, serenity, patience, confidence, and trust.	To advance to the next level, a proficient person needs more experience before s/he can react automatically. S/he must work on cases that matter to him or her so that s/he is motivated to accomplish what needs to be done. Reflection process outlined in section 3 is important if a proficient person finds him or herself in a mood that is not productive. Cultivating moods of ambition and resolution is important to motivate continued practice and learning. Cultivating confidence in ability to learn and a mood of trust in others can be useful for prompting a proficient person to ask for help and seek out mentors and feedback from colleagues.
Expert	An expert is confident in his/her ability to produce positive results and depends almost entirely on intuition. *Moods not conducive to learning:* Arrogance. Also, experts in one domain of expertise often expect themselves to be experts in other domains, and when they find themselves learning something totally new, they may feel very uncomfortable being beginners again. Confusion, frustration, and insecurity can engulf them and prevent them from progressing further in their learning. *Moods conducive to learning:* Wonder, ambition, resolution.	An expert must be willing to override the perspective that as an expert performer s/he intuitively experiences. I.e., s/he forsakes the available appropriate performance and risks regression in performance for the sake of trying a new, less obvious approach. If an expert aspires to be a master, suspension of judgment and a mood of wonder can combat a mood of arrogance that an expert may fall into from time to time. Further, moods of ambition and resolution are important for an expert to cultivate if s/he wants to achieve mastery.
Master	Emotional disposition of a master is aligned with the development of new theories and practices, and making a contribution to his or her field. *Moods not conducive to learning:* Arrogance and resignation may preclude a master from continuing to learn as s/he will be less inclined to ask questions and explore alternatives paths. *Moods conducive to learning:* Generally we would expect to see a person who has achieved a master level of learning to be in a mood of wonder and exploration.	Master is the top level in the learning scale, and if that person is going to take risks and to be willing to override perspectives that s/he intuitively experiences for the sake of experimenting, learning, and innovating, s/he will be more likely to do so if s/he is able to cultivate moods of wonder, ambition, and resolution.

5

WEST: A Virtual Skill Development Laboratory

GAMES AND A NEW ENVIRONMENT FOR LEARNING

As I have already mentioned, a significant inspiration for this book is a four month virtual and fully interactive course we developed six years ago: Working Effectively in Small Teams, (which quickly became the "WEST course" or simply "WEST.") In this course, using an off-the-shelf Multi Player Online Role Playing game (MMORPG), among other things, we developed a laboratory for the development of communication and leadership skills. I will say more shortly about the particular skill-set we focus on in WEST, but for now suffice it to say that prior to designing the first pilot in 2009, my colleagues and I were confident that we could help people develop these skills as we have worked with many clients in organizations do precisely that over the course of many years. However, we had never done this work virtually in a video game setting, and we were not sure how emotionally engaged participants would be as they worked together to complete quests in a game that had absolutely nothing to do with their real lives.

Acquiring these skills, like the acquisition of any skill, is a process that takes emotional engagement, recurrent practice, time, and the navigation of emotional dispositions that may derail us from achieving our objectives. These skills cannot be acquired by sitting in a classroom or a workshop. Real life, of course, is a great place to practice, but it can be risky, particularly in an organization, since we will inevitably make mistakes and we may not, for example, want to offend the wrong person. In such a setting, we may be hesitant to practice, and thus our learning process could significantly slow down or stall.

After more than a decade of consulting work, we were pleased with the results our clients were able to achieve as they developed skills that enabled them to become more effective in the way they worked with each other, their customers, and suppliers. However, we bemoaned the amount of time it took our clients to develop these skills, not to mention the extensive travel required to be on site with our clients. One morning, however, my father and collaborator throughout the years, Fernando Flores, became intrigued by MMORPGs. Watching two of his grandsons play one of these games remotely, each in his respective home, he was fascinated by how engaged the two boys were with each other. He heard them discuss roles and strategy and make constant evaluations about what they were doing well and what they were doing wrong so they could try something different next time. As they worked together to accomplish their quests, he also noticed that they experienced a diversity of moods and emotions in a very short time frame. One moment they were screaming in celebration, and a few minutes later they were sighing with disappointment. After exploring these kinds of games a bit more, including playing with his grandchildren for some time, he speculated that MMORPGs could serve as excellent platforms for the embodied learning of skills that are critical for effective teamwork and leadership, including coordination and collaboration, building trust, listening and working cross-culturally, building strong teams committed to a shared purpose, managing moods, and coping with change and uncertainty on an ongoing basis. He thought that we could help people develop the same kinds of skills that we had been helping our clients develop for many years, but in an environment that:

- Felt real and hence provoked emotional engagement.
- Was safe and playful. If your avatar dies during the game it is not a big deal. You can be back in play to try again within a few minutes or less.
- Allowed for recurrent practice over a period of time, so that the learning could be real as well. The recurrent practice over a length of time

modifies your nervous system, and although the game is not real, the learning is.

Admittedly, as a non-gamer at the time, I was a bit skeptical at first, but as we began to look into these games, we concluded that they could be incredibly helpful in the embodied learning of new skills for three fundamental reasons.

First, education is not simply about the transfer of knowledge and the ability to apply concepts. When it comes to acquiring skills, particularly communication and relationship skills, education is about enabling others to take new actions that they were not able to take before. Simply reading or listening to a lecture will not enable one to embody these skills. They require interaction. In order to learn to coordinate more effectively, we must actively coordinate with one another. In order to learn to build trust, we must actually engage in attempting to do so. In order to learn to observe and manage our moods, we must experience them and take action to attempt to shift them when necessary. MMORPGs provide players with many opportunities for this kind of active practice, because they require players to interact as they work together to get things done.

Second, as the Dreyfus brothers argue, in order for someone to acquire new skills successfully s/he must be emotionally engaged. A person must be involved. He or she must care about producing results. The experience of success and failure is important. And as anyone who plays – or who has watched others play – will be quick to attest, these games can provoke a roller coaster of moods and emotions within a short time frame. As they play with their team members to accomplish their goals, people experience frustration, impatience, confusion, resignation, mistrust, elation, ambition, resolution, and many other moods and emotions, just like in real life. The moods and emotions experienced by members of a team will often make the difference as to whether or not their team is successful, or whether people can forge a collaborative relation. These games can be part of great learning laboratories not only by provoking these moods and emotions, but also by providing an environment where we can learn to observe them and take action to shift them when the situation calls for it.

Finally, all real learning leads to a reformulation of your body's dispositions and tendencies toward certain patterns of behavior, a reformulation that requires recurrent cycles of interaction. To reiterate, learning is a process, and it takes time. Learning new skills, particularly the kinds of skills that we are focused on helping our clients develop, requires repeated exposure to circumstances in which these skills are needed, as well as unlearning certain habits that we have developed over time. Such learning requires practice and more practice. By allowing players to experience situations that feel real to them, and similar to what they experience in real life, but where the consequences of making mistakes are low, MMORPGs can serve as a rich platform for recurrent practice in short time frames, and hence can help produce embodied learning at an accelerated pace.

As a consequence of my father's initial insights about games, we designed and offered our first pilot in 2009, and happily, our speculation that a well-designed learning environment that included a digital game platform could enable learning turned out to be correct. We were excited by the results achieved by the first round of participants in 2009 and have continued to offer it a couple of times a year ever since.

In WEST, as mentioned, we combine an off-the-shelf game, *World of Warcraft*, with:

- A rich framework for participants to observe themselves in action as they work together with others; [36]
- Spaces for reflection so they can explore their assessments about what worked and what did not work, and speculate what they could do different next time; and

---

36 For more on this framework, see the next sections of the book. Also see Fernando Flores, *Conversations for Action and Collected Essays.*

- Spaces for guided and repeated practice where they can take action that may be uncomfortable for them to take, but that is necessary for them to take so that they can learn and acquire the skills that they want to acquire.

During a typical course, we start by forming teams of four or five people with diverse backgrounds – different professions, different cultures, different countries – who may or may not know each other, and ask them to work together to complete certain objectives or missions in the game that by our design will inevitably put them in situations where they may not know what to do or how to do what they may need to do. By putting them in these situations, and by providing them with subsequent spaces for guided discussions and reflection, participants begin to observe their moods, assessments, and standards for learning—the first step in learning to learn. Although the WEST course is focused on developing communication and leadership skills, like skills for coordination, listening, and building trust, we quickly discovered that the key to participants' successfully developing these particular skills is their ability to stay open and predisposed to continued learning.

As they work with their teams, participants quickly discover areas of strengths and areas where they may be stuck or where they need to develop their abilities. They find themselves in situations where they are either complete beginners or somewhere else on the learning scale, but where they need to engage with others and practice together to produce their desired results and achieve their learning objectives.

As you can imagine, and as you will see in some of the case studies I share with you next, the journey towards achieving their learning objectives is not always a smooth one. *I am an accomplished engineer, but I have never encountered anything as difficult as learning to get on the same page and to build trust with my team!* Participants in this course see the value of learning to work more effectively with other people and are committed to further developing what some refer to as "soft skills" – skills that many agree are crucial for today's workforce, but that seem to be in short supply.[37]   Despite their desire to learn, they often face what I call *emotional learning stumbling blocks*.   They fall into moods that are not productive to learning.   A few examples:

- Some want to learn to delegate, but they fall into a mood of resignation about their ability to become good at it because they have the assessment that they should not ask for help or that they should not ask others to do work that they can do themselves. Instead of practicing making requests of their team members, they stay quiet and try to do it all by themselves.
- Some want to learn to grow strong teams around them, but fall into moods of impatience and frustration when their team members don't do what they expect them to do. Instead of taking action to continue to build their teams, they give up and start doing the work on their own. *Teamwork is overrated!*
- Some want to learn to build trust but find themselves in moods of distrust and resignation that keep them from taking the action they need to take to begin to build or rebuild trust. *Building trust is important but I don't trust my colleague's reaction, so I am not going to say what I really think.*
- Some want to further develop their leadership skills, but instead of practicing with their teams, they become anxious about making mistakes or leading the team to failure. When the opportunity to practice leading comes to them, they would rather pass.
- Some want to learn to play their role in the game so they can contribute to their team's success, but instead of enjoying being a beginner, they fall into moods of confusion and resignation because they think they should already know how to play and they don't. Instead of asking for

---

37 *See*, for example, Kate Davidson, "Employers Find 'Soft' Skills Like Critical Thinking In Short Supply" (*The Wall Street Journal*, August 30, 2016). See also Simon Torkington, "The Jobs of the Future – and Two Skills You Need to Get Them" (World Economic Forum, September 2, 2016). Citing David Deming, associate professor of education and economics at Harvard University, the author states that "soft skills like sharing and negotiating" are crucial in the modern workplace. For more on the skill-set we focus on developing in the WEST course, please see the next section.

help and continuing to practice so that they can learn, they lack confidence in their ability to learn, feel embarrassed, and start to disengage.

The good news is that if we learn to shift out of unproductive moods, all of these skills can be learned. Falling into unproductive moods is often a regular occurrence during the learning process, but by learning to observe ourselves falling into moods that may be unproductive to learning, and exploring the assessments that we are making, often automatically, that may trigger those moods, we are then free to explore actions we can take to cultivate alternative moods that are more conducive to learning and to ultimately accomplishing what we care about accomplishing.

Here are three examples of past participants learning to shift out of unproductive moods so that they could continue to learn. In other words, they learned to learn.

Learning to Learn Case Studies[38]

➤ Case Study #1: Allowing yourself to become a beginner
"I am bad at all games. I am not even going to try to learn this one. I don't want to look stupid."

(From anxiety, insecurity and resignation about the possibility of learning to moods of self-confidence and ambition about being a beginner again.)

Robert, a successful media expert, participated in our Working Effectively in Small Teams course. He joined a team with four other people, and we asked them to perform exercises that involved the completion of different quests in *World of Warcraft*. No one in the team had any experience with this game, or with any multiplayer online game.

---

38 Although all of these case studies are based on real examples, the names have been changed to respect people's privacy.

Understandably, they were a bit uncomfortable getting into the game due to their lack of familiarity with it. Shortly afterwards, however, all except Robert began to take action to learn a little about their avatar and the role that they were supposed to play in their team. They came to us and asked questions like: What can my avatar do? What powers does it have? What keys do I need to press? What weapon do I use? What am I supposed to do in this team? Attack or heal? They practiced in the game a little bit, and as they practiced, new questions emerged. What is this new button for? I have a new spell, but how do I use it? When should I use it? As questions arose, or when they got stuck, they either asked our staff, or each other, for help, and within a couple of weeks, spending only a couple of hours a week doing in-game team exercises, everyone but Robert had a grasp of the basic rules of the game, and had moved beyond being a beginner. Robert, on the other hand, announced to the team in their first team meeting that he was no good at games, that he did not like them, and that he was not even going to try to learn because he knew he would be horrible at it. Instead, he said that he would be a cheerleader as they performed their exercises and would facilitate conversations afterwards because, he said, "That's what I am really good at doing."

During the next few team sessions, every time the team met, Robert would say things like "Yay team!" "Good job!" "We will get them next time!" Unbeknownst to Robert, when the team had picked their avatars in the beginning of the course, he picked an avatar that would play the role of tank for the team, a crucial role in the game. A tank is responsible for attracting and retaining a lot of damage, and if the person who assumes that role does not do that, there is very little chance for the team to prevail, no matter how well the others do their job, if they are at a similar level. Since everyone else in the team took the time to learn basic rules and moves, they quickly became aware of the role of the tank and soon grew frustrated with Robert. In a private one-on-one conversation with a member of our staff, one of them complained: "We are never going to be successful because he does not know how to play his role, and he does not even try!"

Although Robert thought he was being helpful by encouraging the team and by otherwise staying out of the way since he was "no good at this game," his encouraging words began to annoy them. Finally one of them said to him: "Your unwillingness to spend an hour working with staff so that they can help you learn a little bit of what you are supposed to do in this game shows that you are not committed to this team at all." Robert was surprised by this comment and responded: "Well, since I am such a beginner, I figure it's best for me to stay out of your way so that the team can win." His teammate responded: "No, you are not a beginner, because a beginner at least commits himself to learning. You haven't done anything, and by not doing anything, you have made sure that we never succeed as a team because the role you are supposed to play is key to our success."

While reflecting upon this with his teammates, Robert explored the assessments that he had that guided his behavior:

- I am not competent at this game, and since I have never been good at games in general, there is no way that I am ever going to be good at this game.
- In order to be a worthy member of the team, it is important to contribute, and since I am not competent, I can't contribute. If I participate, I will hold the team back.
- It is better to step out of the way, and cheer from the sidelines, than to slow the team down. An incompetent person cannot contribute anything.

Becoming aware of his moods, he saw that he was in a mood of resignation about learning these kinds of games, and felt very insecure about his ability to learn to play, particularly since his teammates seemed to be learning. He was anxious about not being able to learn, and decided that it was easier to simply say, "I am not even going to try to learn." As an expert in his field, he was used to people coming to him for answers. He was very uncomfortable not knowing what to do in the game. And further, he also discovered that for him, trying and failing was worse than not trying at all. The latter was less embarrassing.

As he reflected on this with his team, Robert saw that he thought he could participate in something only if he is good at it. In other words, if he is not competent, then he should not participate. He realized that this was an unreasonable expectation to live up to, and that he could play his role of tank as a beginner who follows rules and is told what to do. He saw that no one else in his team expected him to be an expert. They simply wanted him to be a beginner, learn the basic moves of his avatar, and spend a little time working with someone from our staff to orient him to the game and teach him basic tank battle moves.

These realizations helped Robert see how he closed himself to learning anything new for fear of failing and of being embarrassed. In the course, he had closed himself off from the possibility of actually learning to play the game that we used. More importantly, he saw that in real life, there were other opportunities for him to learn new things that he did not pursue.

After this conversation, Robert promised to spend an hour with someone from our staff to get basic training on his avatar and the role that it plays in the game, which he did. Although he did not become an expert tank after one session, he learned enough to be able to engage with his team during their next exercise, and to press a couple of keys on his keyboard during battle. He was excited by the progress that he made after a brief training session and by the progress that the team could make now that he was at least in the game instead of shouting cheers from the sidelines.

Robert and his team enjoyed the few exercises they had left together, and as a result of this experience, Robert was happy to discover that:

- He can learn something new if he resolves to do so.
- It is okay not to be competent at all times. He can participate in new activities as a beginner, and can act accordingly. It is okay not to know how to do something when you are starting out. He can ask for help, and he can coordinate with his teammates as a beginner.

- His moods of anxiety, insecurity, and resignation had shifted, and he now could observe that he was in a mood of confidence about his ability to learn and in a mood of ambition about being a beginner.

➤ Case Study #2: Allowing yourself to be a beginner with others
"I am too old to learn. Technology is for young people."

(From resignation to resolution and ambition.)

Similar to experts, it is not uncommon for older people to feel very uncomfortable in situations where they don't know how to do something. Instead of allowing themselves to learn, they unfortunately decide that it is not for them. "I am too old" is a common assessment underlying a mood of resignation. When exploring this mood, however, often people realize that it is based on standards that do not help them to continue to learn, like "I should be competent and if I am not competent, I should stay out of the way."

One particular example stands out for me as it involves a participant that I admire a lot. Lisa, in her early eighties, was the president and co-founder of a non-profit, and had signed up for the course because she wanted to learn to work in teams more effectively, particularly with volunteer teams. "I have to manage a lot of people who are volunteers and it can be a challenge sometimes as I am not really their boss."

Lisa was a beginner in the game. She was uncomfortable playing at first which was to be expected. There was so much going on in her computer screen that she did not know where to begin. We asked her not to worry about anything in the game other than to practice moving her avatar around. She did, and once she was comfortable doing that, she was ready for the next step in the course: to begin to coordinate with her team while in the game together. When she met with her team to perform their exercises, she got disoriented, got separated from her teammates and felt bad about her performance in the game. She fell into a mood of frustration (she thought she should be able to keep up with her team but she could not) and resignation (she felt that she would never be able to keep up as "technology was for the young.") She called me to say that reluctantly she was going to have to quit the course. She told me:

"I am disappointed as what I am learning here about teams already has helped me outside the course and I have no doubt that I will learn more."

"Perhaps you should continue in the course then," I said to her.

"I would like to stay, but I don't think I should. I don't want to hold my team back. I am sure that at least one of them is frustrated with me because I get lost all of the time. This technology is too hard for me. It's for young people."

"Do you think your team could support you better so that you can play your role? I am sure that you have a lot to contribute to them," I responded.

We talked a bit more, and Lisa promised to think about it for a couple of days even though she was leaning towards quitting. However, when she reflected on the moods she found herself in, and on what she really wanted to learn in the course (how to work more effectively with her teams in real life), she resolved to complete the course and to make requests to her teammates to support her in the game so that she could do her part. She said to me: "There is a lot here for me to learn and I am not quitting just because I get disoriented in the game."

Her teammates were thrilled that she continued to participate with their team. One of them (who originally worried about Lisa holding the team back) said to me: "As a team, we can find ways to support her to play her role. I can easily make sure that she does not get lost, but I can't replace her. She is an incredibly valuable member of this team. It's not every day that I get to learn from someone with so much life experience and I am learning a lot from her."

➢ Case Study #3: Learning to enjoy being a beginner
"I have to show that I know what I am doing right away."

(From frustration, impatience, and insecurity to self-confidence, patience, and trust in others.)

Like Robert, Clara was very successful in her career. She had a masters and a PhD and had up until recently been the editor-in-chief of an important publication. She had also published several books and was a sought after speaker. Prior to enrolling in the WEST course, she launched a new startup venture, and thought that the course could help her be more effective working with teams, something that she had not had to do often in her previous roles. And like Robert, Clara had never played a MMORPG game before and was nervous about playing with other people and doing it right. Unlike Robert, however, she was committed to learning to play, and spent many hours, even before the course started, playing on her own and trying to understand how the game worked so that she could contribute to her team right away.

Clara was assigned to a team of accomplished people, including a CEO of a financial services company, a retired Navy Captain, and a senior manager of a global software company. When she and her team began to meet for their weekly team exercises, they did not accomplish the missions that we gave them. Far from it. Clara found that she often fell behind her team, got lost and/or killed – in the game only, of course – and did not know what to do. Her team members offered her help: "Clara where are you? Stay there, I'll come get you. Right click on my avatar and press follow." Over and over again, however, Clara did not accept their offer for help: "Don't worry, I will find you. I am looking at a map. I am turned around, but I will get there." Alternatively, she would either go silent and not respond to their offers of help, or she would not follow the instructions they gave her. Her team grew increasingly frustrated, and did not know how to help her. "If she does not listen, how can I tell her what she has to do?" one of her exasperated teammates asked in a private conversation. Clara became more frustrated as well. "I should be able to do this," she said. "I have invested hours of my time trying to figure out this game on my own. I think I understand what I am supposed to do, but then when I am in action with the team, I get disoriented and lost."

Her teammates did not know that Clara spent hours on her own trying to master the game. One day, one of them told her that he thought she was not taking her commitment to the course seriously enough because she was not adequately preparing for the team exercises, and asked her to spend an hour or two learning the game so that she would stop holding up the team so much. At that point, Clara became upset with her teammate – she was more than committed to the team and to the course – and shared that she spent many hours practicing on her own. She, in fact, had spent more hours than all of them combined trying to "get up to speed in this silly game," but when she met with them, it did not show. As she explored with her teammates what has happening, Clara realized that she had made the following assessments that perhaps got in the way of her learning:

- My teammates expect me to be competent. I need to show them that I am.
- I should be competent by now given how many hours I have dedicated to learning this game on my own. I should be able to master this faster.

She was very stressed in those first encounters with her team, and wanted to quit. The only reason she did not quit, she said, was because she "was not a quitter." The commitment to persevere helped her stay in the course, but she hated every moment of working with her team. It wasn't fun.

She was frustrated because she expected to be competent in the game and she was not. She felt she should know how to play by now, and was impatient with herself. She felt insecure about her ability to learn the game and succeed in the mission. "Everyone else seems to know what they are doing." She thought that her lack of skill in the game made it a waste of time for her and the team. She thought she should be able to master the game faster. Most importantly, because she thought she needed to be competent, she could not bring herself to say: "I don't know how to do this. Who can help me?" She did not want others to think less of her. She did not trust them to take care of her. She noticed that she could not even hear people's attempts to help or to give her instructions. The more lost she got, the more confused she felt, and the worse she felt. She turned inward, and it never occurred to her that there were other people there, including her teammates, who were willing to help her. Later, reflecting on this with them, she could see that they were indeed exasperated with her, but not because she did not know how to do something, but because she did not allow them to help her.

As a result of this experience, Clara discovered that:

- She had unreasonable expectations of herself. Not only were those expectations not shared by her teammates, they did not help her learn. They only helped her feel frustrated.
- She did not have to be competent right away. It was okay to not know how to do something or to get lost in the game. She could ask others for help. Her teammates were willing to help her. As she became aware of that, Clara resolved to practice saying "I don't know" and asking for help, instead of always trying to figure things out on her own. She asked her teammates to give her feedback and to point out when she was not listening. They agreed to do so.

As the next few weeks unfolded, Clara continued to prepare herself more than other participants, but she did not expect herself to be competent in the game. At the end of the fourth week or so, Clara began to relax, to ask for help when she did not know what to do, and to actually listen to her teammates' questions and instructions. She began to trust her capacity to learn with her team, and to trust her team and their care for her. Her mood of frustration went away. She was patient with herself when she found that she was stuck, but instead of going silent, she asked for help. As a result, she was able to enjoy herself in the game and to learn to play with others much faster than on her own. Consequently, her team became much more successful in completing the in-game missions that we assigned them.

➤ Case Study #4: Learning to learn beyond expert
"I am the expert here and it is my responsibility to tell people what to do."

(Shifting mood of arrogance to mood of wonder and exploration)

Pat, a consultant, seasoned gamer, and expert in *World of Warcraft* in real life, was assigned to a team comprised of people who had never played such games before.

During their first few exercises, the team was very efficient in completing the missions we asked them to complete. Pat's team members, who had initially been very anxious about playing the game since they had zero experience with it prior to the course, were thrilled to have an expert among them. They were happy to take instructions from Pat and to do whatever he told them to do. One team member said: "I was so stressed about playing this game as I had no clue what to do, and I am so relieved that Pat is on my team and tells us what to do." As the weeks passed, however, and Pat's team members got more experienced in the game, they began to ask questions and to offer alternative strategies to the ones he proposed. Without fail, Pat shot down their proposals. "That might be a good idea, but this is what we have to do and how we have to do it. Trust me, I have done this a few times. This is the best way to do it."

Eventually the strategy of "It's Pat's way or no way" stumbled. We had asked the team to travel to an island to get a giant turtle. Up to that point, we had not assigned anything that required them to swim under water, but getting to the turtle would likely require it, unless they came up with something different. Swimming in *World of Warcraft* is not a big deal; it is almost like walking, but for adults that have never played the game before, it can be disorienting because they don't see any landmarks and they don't know that they can hold their breath under water. It can also be stress-provoking, because even though it isn't real, it *feels* real, and they don't want to drown.

Pat had been in this part of the game before, and knew exactly what to do. "Let's swim across," he commanded. His team obliged. Within a few moments, chaos ensued. A few of his teammates got disoriented and got lost, others came under attack by creatures swimming underwater and their avatars died. After getting back to the starting point again, Pat asked them to follow the same strategy and explained where they were going. Chaos resulted once again. A bit frazzled but confident that his was the only way to do it, he reassured a team member who asked if there might be a different way to get the turtle. "Trust me, this is how we have to do it." After a few more attempts using the same strategy, the same team member who asked earlier if there might be another way to do it remembered a strategy they had used in a prior exercise where they had attacked a target from a distance, and the targeted creature had then ran towards them. "That won't work here," Pat said for some reason. They tried Pat's strategy once again without success, and thankfully the team member insisted and asked if they could try the strategy that they had used in a prior exercise. "What's the worst that can happen?" Feeling defeated, Pat ceded, and the team member tried a new strategy, a strategy that would rarely, if ever, be tried by an experienced gamer in the same situation, because she or he would know, as Pat did, how to swim and use the map in the game. Lo and behold, the strategy worked. No one other than Pat got in the water, and the rest of the team supported him by attacking from the comfortable and familiar dry land. Mission accomplished.

Upon reflecting on their experience, Pat could see that he had fallen into moods of arrogance and frustration. He saw that he automatically made the following assessments:

- I am an expert in this game. I know all there is to know, and even though others may have different ideas, they just need to listen to me. I know how to do it.
- My team should listen to me and should be able to do what I am asking them to do.

As he explored these assessments, Pat began to see that even though he thought his team should do what he thought they should do, in this case, they were unable to do so, and he had not known how to effectively guide them.

Although he might have been able to give instructions to people who could execute them, when working with a team of beginners, he did not know how to lead them to success. Pat also saw that instead of making assessments about the situations they found themselves in for the sake of coming up with a strategy that could work, he kept pushing the same unsuccessful strategy over and over again, becoming increasingly frustrated by their failure. He was surprised that it took someone with less experience in the game to devise a strategy that could be executed by people with less experience.

As a result of this exercise, Pat began to see how a mood of arrogance limited him from exploring different ways of doing things with other people who might not have as much experience, but who might see things that he does not. He began to practice asking more questions. He learned to evaluate situations from the perspective of beginners like his teammates, and he began to see ways of doing things in the game that he had not seen before. The team began to take on more responsibility, and regularly came up with effective strategies for completing the missions we assigned them, which allowed Pat to continue learning without the self-imposed pressure of always knowing what to do. Pat began to see the possibility of continuing to learn and of achieving mastery, and not being stuck as the expert who knows the only right way to do something. By shifting from a mood of arrogance to one of wonder and exploration, Pat saw that not knowing something was an opportunity to explore new questions and learn something new. It did not have to be a source of frustration.

6

Acquiring Other Skills: Further WEST Case Studies

During our delivery of the WEST course, we found that a core aspect of our students' success in developing the skills that they sought to develop was the emotional disposition they found themselves in during the learning process. Hence, while we repeatedly exposed students to situations in which the skills they wanted to develop were needed so that they could practice, we also helped them become aware of moods they fell into that got in the way of their learning, and supported them in taking action to shift out of them so that they could continue to learn.

In this part of the book, I share a few more case studies that show how WEST participants were able to learn to learn, and as a result, were able to develop other valuable skills. Before diving into these, however, I provide a bit more context by describing the specific skill-set we help participants develop in WEST, and a few words about the underlying design principles of the course.

SKILL-SET DEVELOPED IN WEST
We live in a global, networked age, allowing us to connect to a diversity of people all over the world. But, in the words of the psychologist Paul Ekman, a world-renowned expert on the science of emotions, "...although we are all the same, we are also all different...in what we inherit and in what we learn."[39] And, not surprisingly, we do not yet know how to live

---

39 Ekman, *Emotional Awareness*, 45.

together in pluralistic networks: networks in which people of different backgrounds, nationalities, cultures, and belief systems commit to living and working together, respecting differences, and collaborating to create value for each other. There are many challenges to doing this. There is often great distrust between people. In similar situations, we may react in very dissimilar fashions. We have different expectations, different standards of behavior, and different attitudes that dictate what we see as appropriate or inappropriate, and as possible or not possible. If we believe that other people can't understand us, or are too different from us, we may give up on working together at the first sign of conflict, whether it is an outsourcing contract between international teams, or an interdepartmental project being executed by people from different professional backgrounds. If we cannot surmount those challenges, our ability to collaborate and innovate will be adversely affected.

Teams need new skills that will enable people to work more effectively together. Among these are the:

- Ability to coordinate our commitments.
- Ability to learn together and to listen for concerns by making and exploring assessments.
- Ability to build trust and repair trust when it is broken.
- Ability to observe and manage background moods.
- Ability to cultivate *emotional fortitude*, the capacity to cope with change and disturbances on an ongoing basis.

This is the skill set that we introduce to WEST participants.[40] Although these skills are regularly intertwined, we help them to develop each one of these by continuously focusing their attention on communication building blocks: how we coordinate action, how we make and listen to assessments, and how we fall into moods that open and close possibilities for us.   I share a few case studies below, but first a few more words on the design of the course.

GUIDING DESIGN PRINCIPLES FOR WEST
Three guiding principles underlie the design of the curriculum and the delivery of this course.

First, successful communication between people is expressed in the successful coordination of commitments. Human beings invent their world through language. In his groundbreaking dissertation, Fernando Flores, drawing and expanding upon the tradition of "speech act theory" initiated by John Austin and further developed by John Searle, claimed that there is a universal (no matter what country you go to, these will be there) yet finite set of conversational moves that people make, or can make, when coordinating their commitments with one another:

---

40 This is our working definition of the soft skills required for working with others in today's world. Often others have slightly different definitions. For example, *The Wall Street Journal* recently said that companies across the United States say it is becoming increasingly difficult for companies to find candidates "who can communicate clearly, take initiative, problem-solve and get along with co-workers." They say that "[w]hile such skills have always appealed to employers, decades-long shifts in the economy have made them especially crucial now. Companies have automated or outsourced many routine tasks, and the jobs that remain often require workers to take on broader responsibilities that demand critical thinking, empathy or other abilities that computers can't easily simulate," (Davidson, "Employers Find 'Soft Skills' Like Critical Thinking in Short Supply"). In its *Future of Jobs* Report, the World Economic Forum lists 10 top skills identified by senior executives and top human resources managers across industries and across developed and emerging economies. These include, among others: people management, ability to coordinate with others, emotional intelligence, good judgment decision making skills, service orientation, and negotiation and cognitive flexibility, (*The Future of Jobs* 21). We are confident that the skills that we focus on developing during the WEST course are foundational to the development of the types of skills mentioned by these two organizations. *The Wall Street Journal* mentions that employers are somewhat resigned about the ability to find people with these skills: "of nearly 900 executives last year, 92% said soft skills were equally important or more important than technical skills. But 89% said they have a very or somewhat difficult time finding people with the requisite attributes." The good news, however, is that these are not fixed attributes of people. They are skills that can be developed, and we can embark on a process of doing just that if we want to do so.

Request: A Speaker asks a Listener to take care of something the Speaker is concerned about.

Offer/Promise: A Speaker offers or promises to take care of something that the Listener is concerned about.

Assess: A Speaker assesses how some action or thing relates to specific concerns or commitments.

Assert: A Speaker asserts (reports) facts pertinent to the concern at hand.

Declaration: A Speaker declares a new world of possibilities for action in a community.

How these various speech acts show up, or are available to people, may vary, however, and a key focus of the WEST course is focused on developing our participants' ability to observe these moves – how they are made and not made – and consequently, to develop their ability to coordinate more effectively with one another.[41]

Second, listening has to do with exploring the concerns of other people and being predisposed to take care of these. Hence, a significant focus of the four months of work in teams is the exploration of how we listen to each other, and how we explore concerns, even if these concerns are not explicitly articulated. How we make, listen, and explore assessments is a key aspect of this.

Finally, and perhaps most relevant to this book, all action, including learning, occurs in an emotional space. Moods are pervasive, influencing us at all times, and they predispose us to different possibilities. If I have seen a lot of change initiatives in my company that never amounted to anything, I may feel resigned and cynical, and reluctant to collaborate with those leading the latest efforts. I am not going to make offers and I am not going to make requests, even though those moves are available to me. If I do not think it is

---

41 For more on this, see Fernando Flores and Terry Winograd, *Understanding Computers and Cognition* (Norwood, NJ: Ablex Publ., 1987), particularly Chapter 5. See also, Flores, *Conversations for Action and Collected Essays*.

appropriate to ask for help, I will be resigned about my ability to delegate, no matter how much sense it makes to do so.

Accordingly, our work on teams explores moods, and increases people's ability to navigate these effectively so they can accomplish their team objectives. Learning to navigate moods that get in the way of learning to coordinate our commitments and to listen is crucial to us successfully learning to do so.

DEVELOPING COORDINATION SKILLS

The speech acts mentioned above are universal. It does not matter whether you are in China or the United States or Brazil. If you want someone to do something, you have to make a request. (Sometimes we wish people could read our minds, but that is unlikely to happen.) If you would like to do something for someone else, you will make an offer. Nothing happens between two people unless one of these two moves is made. The successful coordination of action between people starts with a request or an offer. If team members are not making offers and requests to each other, that team is probably not collaborating well.

This sounds simple enough, but how speech acts are made, and what sort of receptivity people have for each of them, varies from country to country, culture to culture, and even person to person. We have different histories. We have different educational backgrounds. We have acquired different social norms and standards throughout our lives. We respond differently to situations. What may be acceptable to someone from California may not be acceptable to someone from Shanghai. What may be appropriate to someone from engineering may not be acceptable to someone from marketing. Our lives shape what we consider possible or not, acceptable or not, without us even being aware of it.

In our work, we see that people quickly understand that we invent our world with others in language using this finite set of conversational moves. Yet when it comes to making these moves in action with others, they often stumble. They would like help from someone, but they can't bring themselves to ask. They have a great idea for the team, but they can't bring themselves to make an offer, or they make an offer that no one accepts. They have assessments about the way someone else is performing his or her role in a way that may be detrimental to a project's success, but they don't make them publicly. Something holds them back. They find themselves in moods that are not conducive to working with teams, or to reaching their objectives: frustration, resignation, and distrust. Instead of accomplishing their goals, they start to disengage and eventually give up.

The possibility of failing as a team is reduced as we learn to make and listen for these moves. This requires that we become aware of moods that keep us from making and listening for these moves, like arrogance or resignation; it requires that we explore the assessments we have about the situation, and that we discover the standards guiding our behavior. We may need to modify or abandon standards that hinder our ability to successfully coordinate action with others. We must practice making conversational moves, even those that make us uncomfortable, particularly as we unlearn self-defeating habits and behavior. With recurrent practice and time, however, we can develop these skills and become much more effective in the way we work with other people.

Learning to Make Effective Requests

If we want someone to do something, we have to make a request. During the WEST course, participants read about the key elements of a request:[42]

1. A Speaker – Someone makes a request.
2. A Listener – A request is made to someone specific.
3. Conditions of fulfillment – What do you want done? How?
4. Background of obviousness – The Speaker and the Listener have similar backgrounds for understanding the request.
5. Time – Specified time for fulfillment of the request.
6. Request – Action to be performed in the future by the Listener.

These elements seem obvious, but there are numerous situations in which a request may be warranted but no one makes it – there is no speaker of the request – and the opportunity for coordination is lost. Often, we share information with people, but we don't make any requests that would allow us to coordinate action with one another to accomplish anything. During the course, students in the game may say, "I am lost," but they don't ask for someone to come find them or to guide them back to the team. A student running late to a team meeting may send a text or an e-mail to the rest of the

---

42 See Flores, *Conversations for Action and Collected Essays* previously mentioned.

team stating "I am running late," but he/she doesn't make a request to the team that could guide what they do about the meeting. Should they wait? Should they start without the person running late? Should they reschedule? In that situation, for the sake of more effective coordination, making a request is more helpful than just letting them know that he/she will be late. The student could ask the team to wait for them, or to start without them, or to reschedule. The absence of that request leaves the rest of the team at a loss as to what to do, leading to wasted time, frustration, and breaks in trust.[43]

What stops us from making requests? Perhaps we simply don't know that a request is a move we can make. Perhaps due to culture, family, or social class, we don't have much practice making requests; once we become aware of that, we can practice making more of them. Often, however, we don't feel comfortable making requests. We understand that we *can* make a request, but we don't. We have assessments that get in the way. Similar to the assessments that get in the way of learning, we have assessments that persuade us that it is not okay to ask for help or that we should not make a request. Consequently, instead of making requests, we fall into negative moods that hinder us from even seeing requests as possible moves. Exploring those assessments and modifying the standards that give rise to them is key to enabling us to learn to make requests and to delegate.

➤ Case Study #5: Learning to delegate and ask for help
"Asking for help is not appropriate. I must do things by myself."

(From frustration, resignation, insecurity, and distrust to self-confidence, trust, and resolution.)

---

43 Of course, in the absence of such a request, a team member could step up and make an offer that would take care of his/her team member and the rest of the team, but in this situation, no one did, which also led to interesting reflections.

Ann, a senior manager at a global corporation, enrolled in WEST without a particular learning objective at first. She felt that she worked pretty well in teams, but was open to strengthening her skills. She was very busy at work and felt that perhaps if she was more effective in how she worked with others, she could have a more balanced life. We assigned her to a team where she was the only woman, something that she was used to in her teams at work. Immediately, Ann took the lead in convening the team, scheduling work times, and in offering technology assistance to her team members. She started practicing on her own prior to the course officially starting and offered to help her team members if they needed anything.

During their second exercise, we sent the team of five to an area in the game that would require significant coordination. There was a high probability that a few of them would get lost, or come under attack by non-player characters (aka "NPC" or computer generated enemies) that were at a much higher level than the players' avatars. We asked them to spend no more than an hour traveling to a particular destination in the game, but we knew that chances of any of them being able to get there were slim unless they traveled as a group and supported each other if any of them came under attack.

Shortly after the exercise started, Ann, the designated leader for that exercise, was attacked by a bear, but did not let her team members know. She tried to fight the bear on her own, but not surprisingly, her avatar was killed. In the game, being killed is only a momentary inconvenience as you come back to life quickly. But Ann found herself separated from her team members with very little idea how to make her way back to them. The rest of the team moved ahead and had no idea what was happening to her. A few minutes went by and finally one of them noticed that he did not see her and asked how she was doing because he did not see her.

"I got killed, you guys. I am sorry. I tried to defend myself but it did not work. I am making my way back. I am sorry."

Five to 10 minutes later, another team member asked her how she was doing. Sounding very frustrated, she responded:

"I am so sorry, I am trying to get back to you, but I keep getting killed. So sorry for holding you up."

A few minutes later, she was asked once again how she was doing, and with more frustration in her voice,

"I am sorry you guys. I am so frustrated. I feel awful for holding the team up. I am still trying but maybe you should go on without me."

When reminded that the mission required everyone in the team to arrive at the destination, she once again apologized for holding everyone up. A few minutes later, time was up. They had failed to complete their mission, and Ann felt guilty for not knowing how to get back to her team members and causing them to fail.

"I am sorry. I was not a very good leader today! We failed because I could not get back to you."

Immediately after the exercise was over, the team spent some time reflecting on their experiences. Prior to this meeting, we had assigned a reading to the team about Conversations for Action, and in particular about requests. When I asked Ann if she ever considered requesting help since she did not know how to travel and reunite with her teammates, she told me that she thought about asking for help for a second but immediately discarded that idea and tried to figure out how to do it on her own. When we explored a little more about why she wouldn't ask for help, she said, "I don't want to be the weakest link of the team. It is important that I do my part, and that I not bother my colleagues who are busy with their own stuff." Never mind that they were all sitting at their keyboards simply waiting for her. When members of her team heard her say that she felt like the weakest link on the team, they expressed surprise. They said they felt she was always a leader on the team, and that they really valued how she had brought the team together and how much help she had given each one of them at various times. They all agreed that they absolutely would not have thought any less of her had she said, "I don't know how to get back. I need help. Can someone tell me what to do?"

Upon reflection, Ann saw that she found herself in at least three different moods during the exercise:

1. Frustration: She wanted to successfully complete the mission with her team, but she could not get back to the team once she got separated from the other team members, and as a result, they could not reach the assigned destination.
2. Resignation: Ann wanted to accomplish the mission and to get back to her team members, but since she could not figure out how to get back to them without getting killed, despite trying multiple times, she started to give up. She did not see anything she could do that would allow the team to succeed.
3. Distrust/Insecurity: She realized that she did not know how to get back to her team, but she felt that if she asked, the team would assess her as weak. If she asked for help, they would not think that she was competent to be on the team. She also saw herself as the weakest link.

Upon further reflection, Ann discovered that several assessments and under-lying standards guided her actions and prevented her from asking for help, which also prevented the team from learning to travel and from successfully completing their mission:

- It is important to always know the answers. If you don't, then others will think that you are incompetent or stupid. It is bad to be incompe-tent or stupid.
- If you don't know the answer, stay out of the way. Be quiet so that people don't think you are stupid and lose interest in working with you.

- One must not be a burden to others. Everyone is responsible for him or herself. If you don't know how to do something, figure it out yourself.
- It is wrong to ask for help. Everyone is responsible for his or herself. Asking for help bothers others who are already busy enough with their own stuff.

She also recognized that the situation she found herself in during the exercise happened to her regularly in real life. At work, if she did not know how to do something, she often did not delegate or ask for help, but simply buckled down and tried to figure out how to do it herself. As in this exercise with her team, this left her feeling frustrated and overwhelmed. She worked long hours but still could not get to everything. She felt resentful of the colleagues who worked fewer hours, without offering their help. She was also resigned about the possibility of asking for help because she believed that it was not appropriate for her to do so. As she saw it, her only options were to work longer hours, be stressed and overwhelmed, or to quit.

Publically admitting that she did not know how to do something and asking for help did not come easy for Ann. She came from the south, from a family who believed that a woman should focus on being a homemaker and not on having a career. Working in an environment where she was often the only woman in a male-dominated field, her assessments of appropriate or inappropriate behavior on her part were deeply ingrained. She believed that she always had to prove that she belonged at work and that she was just as competent, if not more competent, than her male colleagues. Holding on to this belief kept her from asking for help or from delegating in situations where that would have been the best solution.

After this exercise, she saw that her assessments and underlying standards for what is appropriate behavior got in the way of her learning. She also realized that by not asking for help, she had actually hurt the team instead of relieving it of the burden of helping her. She began to see that saying "I don't know" is not a sign of weakness, but rather an assessment that can lead to more effective participation in the team. Allowing herself to say "I want/need to learn" and then to ask for help, or to determine "I don't need to know this" and then to delegate the task to someone else, left her free to focus on other matters instead of spending hours trying to figure things out on her own.

When Ann realized that the standards she had set for herself actually held her and the team back, she resolved to practice asking for help during her team exercises. The more she did it, the easier it became, an ease that began to translate to her real life as well. She was able to successfully shift moods that were not conducive to accomplishing her objectives. She moved from frustration, overwhelm, insecurity, and resignation, to self-confidence and resolution. She resolved to learn to ask for help and to delegate more, and although it was not comfortable at first, she continued to practice with her team in the course and with her colleagues at work. Less than a year after she participated in this course, she was promoted at work and given much more responsibility. She credited her promotion to her increased ability to ask for help and delegate, instead of trying to figure everything out on her own.[44]

➤ Case Study #6: Learning to build a strong team and to delegate effectively "It's a waste of time to delegate if people are not competent. I will end up having do the work myself."

(From arrogance, frustration, impatience, and distrust to trust, ambition and resolution.)

Daniel, a construction company executive, signed up for our Working Effectively in Small Teams course in part because he wanted to learn to lead in a different manner. "I tend to be top-down, and I would like to develop

44 Ann is not alone when it comes to her ability to delegate. As mentioned earlier in this book, according to a 2015 Gallup Poll, only one in four employer entrepreneurs have a high degree of what they call "Delegator talent," which they see as key to business growth and expansion. The more someone is able to delegate, the more likely his or her business will grow. (Badel and Ott, "Delegating: A Huge Management Challenge for Entrepreneurs.")

a more collaborative style of leadership," he told us. As we began to work together, we discovered that Daniel did not delegate effectively, and that he quickly fell into moods that were not conducive to learning to do so, or to fulfilling his objective of developing a more collaborative style of leadership. Here is how he was able to reach his learning objective.

Daniel, an experienced gamer, was assigned to a team of five people, and every time he met with his team during the first few exercises, he was quick to point out that the clock was ticking and that they needed to take action in the game. His team members, none of whom had experience with *World of Warcraft*, wanted to talk about the week's mission, their roles, how they were going to do it, and about each of their learning objectives so they could support each other during gameplay. In contrast, Daniel wanted to spend less time talking and instead wanted to quickly jump into the mission. Whenever it was his turn to lead, he would simply tell his team what they needed to do and then jump into action without much discussion. He became frustrated because they were not able to accomplish missions that he knew from experience were very easy. In a one-on-one conversation with me, he asked, "Why don't they do what I ask of them? I give them pretty simple instructions."

As we explored the situation, Daniel asked if he could change teams. He could not understand how, despite telling his team members what to do, they still failed to execute. Among other things, he said things like, "The missions are not hard. I've done them plenty of times by myself. Any 12-year-old can do them."

As we talked, he became aware of two moods he was in that might have been preventing him from learning to build a strong team: Impatience and Arrogance. He already knew what needed to be done, and his teammates' desire to talk, talk, talk, was a waste of time. There was no value, as far as he could see, in their conversations because talking just delayed them from completing the task at hand. He also was in a mood of distrust about the team as they were incompetent to do what young children could do.

As we explored these moods, he began to see how they were not conducive to learning to build a strong team. He saw that he was very focused on completing the mission, but not focused on learning to build a strong team, which is what he really wanted to learn to do. As we explored his assessments about the team's competence, he realized that:

- His team was not competent in the game, but they could learn some basic things so that they could perform their respective roles.
- Unless every member of the team increased his or her competence, the team would never achieve its missions because each member had a crucial role to play to make that happen. A team without a good healer (the person who generally protects the health of team members), for example, is less likely to succeed, as is a team without a good tank, since that person has better armor and can take more damage from an enemy.
- He could not play all of the roles himself, despite knowing how to play them, and if his teammates could not execute, it did not matter what he knew. He could not do it for them and the team would fail.

As he reflected further, he realized that his teammates' desire to talk was connected to them not knowing much about the game. They were just trying to figure out what each member was supposed to be doing, and had very little understanding of their respective roles within the team. He could see that simply telling them to attack would not necessarily lead to good results if the attackers did not know when and how to do so, and if those who were supposed to heal did not know their role. As he reflected on his assessments and his expectation that people had to be competent right away, Daniel realized that the standards that he was adhering to did not enable him to build a strong team. As a leader, he saw that completing the task at hand was important, but so was training team members so that they could fulfill their roles. Falling into frustration whenever they did not perform was not going to produce a strong team.

After exploring the underlying assessments behind his moods, Daniel resolved to train his team so that they could be successful, and felt ambitious about doing so. He offered to hold a training session, which his team members gladly accepted, and also proposed a couple of new practices, including a 10 to 15 minutes check-in before each session to talk briefly about the week's mission and their roles, and to see if there were any questions or requests for help. As a result, after just two work sessions, he felt that he could trust his teammates to play their respective roles, and that he did not have to tell them exactly what to do because they knew what they had to do. If they did not, he invited them to ask questions, and he promised to make the time to listen. He reported being much more relaxed, and was thrilled that they were more successful as a team in their subsequent assignments. Afterwards, whenever it was his turn to lead, he reported that he really enjoyed that he "had so little to do."

Not surprisingly, the situation Daniel encountered during the course with his team was similar to what he was experiencing in real life with his team at work. He said that he was frustrated with his team because he often found their work to be below his expectations, and rather than helping them fix things that he assessed as subpar, or even asking them to do something in the first place, he would do the work himself, which limited how much he could do, and how many deals they could go after. Daniel could see that he hesitated to delegate to people that reported to him, and that often he simply chose not to. "What is the point?" Daniel asked. "It is going to come back to me anyway and it will take much less time if I just do it myself."

Daniel observed himself in the following moods:

- Frustration: He wanted to be able to delegate more so that he could be free to do other things that required his attention, but whenever he asked someone on his team to do something, it did not meet his standards and he had to do it over, wasting more time.
- Distrust: He did not think that his team was competent to do what he needed them to do. They did not have his experience, and as such, they did not perform up to his expectations.

- Resignation: He did not think there was anything else he could do about it. The work had to be done, and if his team was not competent, he simply had to do it himself and postpone or give up on other things that needed his attention.[45]
- Impatience: He felt that delegating to his team when he knew that he was just going to have to do it over again himself was a waste of time. There was no value in delegating.

As a result of what he experienced in the program, Daniel could see that the assessments underlying the moods he found himself in were not well grounded or helpful to his goal of building a stronger team. If his team was not competent, and he did not take the time to train them, then they would never become more competent. Perhaps spending a little more time training his team, reviewing their work, and asking them to redo the work instead of doing it himself would help his team members learn and eventually assume more responsibility. He became ambitious to help the people in his team grow, and he resolved to do so. Among other things, he introduced new practices at his work that allowed him to regularly listen to the people that reported to him, discuss the results that they needed to produce together, and talk about each other's roles in bringing about those results.

After the course, he told us that he was in fact becoming successful in developing a more inclusive and collaborative style at work, and that as a result, the people that reported to him were moving strongly without him. Just a few months later they were able to make a successful multi-million dollar sales pitch completely without his involvement. He was happy and freed up to do other projects that he previously did not have time to do, and the people who reported to him were happy as they felt more supported by him than

---

45 Coincidentally, when exploring his team members' moods, Daniel could also see that they shared a mood of distrust and frustration too. His team was also frustrated because they wanted to take on more responsibility and grow in their careers, but did not feel that Daniel was giving them that opportunity. They did not trust that Daniel was taking care of supporting their career development.

when he had simply taken over their work and done it himself. By reflecting on the moods that kept him from delegating effectively and developing a more collaborative and inclusive style of leadership, Daniel was able to identify actions he could take that would allow him to continue to grow his team instead of simply giving up or firing the team. By taking those actions, Daniel was able to successfully shift moods of frustration, distrust, resignation, and impatience to moods of trust, resolution and ambition. His learning objective was accomplished.

Ann and Daniel are just two examples of many people who are reluctant to make requests. For Ann, asking for help was not possible; she thought it was not something appropriate for her to do. Without explicitly adopting it, Ann adhered to the standard that she always had to be just as competent, if not more competent, than everyone else. Consequently, she thought she should never ask for help. Daniel did not delegate because he thought that delegating to people who are not competent is not a productive use of time, and rather than waste time, he should just do it himself. Of course, this prevented him from developing the people around him and developing a more collaborative style of leadership, which is what he wanted to learn to do. Other people are not reluctant to make requests. In fact, they make them often, but don't get the actions they want to produce. This can lead to bad moods, damaged team relationships, and failure to meet the team's objectives.

➤ Case Study #7: Learning to make effective requests in a civilian setting "People don't do what I ask. What's the point of working in teams?"

(Shifting frustration, resignation, and distrust to a commitment to building trust and resolving to learn.)

Mike, a senior army officer, wanted to learn to better lead teams in a civilian setting. Unlike the people in the two examples above, Mike did not shy away from making requests. However, he found that often he was unable to produce the action he desired when working with civilian teams. He had spent many years in the military, and he was used to giving orders to people who reported to him and to having those orders fulfilled. In the civilian world he did not have as much success. "I ask people to do something and then they either don't do it at all or they don't do what I ask," he told us.

Not surprisingly, when working with his team in the WEST course, Mike experienced the same thing. He made requests that people seemingly ignored, or tried to fulfill, but not in the manner that Mike wanted. For example, during one of the team exercises that Mike was leading, he asked the team to stay close until they were ready to attack. While they talked about their strategy for bringing down the enemy, one team member innocently walked around the corner, and the team immediately came under attack. The team member attracted – or "aggroed" for those familiar with this game – enemies by getting too close to them, which led the enemies to quickly attack the team and wipe it out. During the debrief, Mike said to his team member: "I asked everyone to stay close, but you didn't."

Upon reflection, Mike observed the following:

- He was in a mood of frustration. He wanted his teammates to do what he asked them to do, but they often did not. He felt particularly frustrated when he felt that had his requests been accepted and fulfilled as he wished, the team would have been more likely to successfully complete their mission. Had his teammate stayed put while they worked out the strategy of attack, they could have defeated the monster. Instead, they all died before they even had a chance to attack.
- He was in a mood of distrust with his teammates. He assessed them as either totally incompetent or not interested in collaborating with him. In this case, he made a very specific request, and one teammate still failed to stay close.
- He was in a mood of resignation. No matter how many times he made requests, chances were that his teammates wouldn't comply. He found himself less willing to make requests and less willing to engage with

his team. "I am trying, but somehow I can't get them to do what I ask," he said. "This was a great example. I made a clear request and my teammate did not do what I asked."

As Mike began to reflect on these moods, he could see that they were not conducive to effectively collaborating with his team, or to learning to make effective requests and leading in a civilian setting. Quite the opposite, the moods of frustration, distrust, and resignation made him want to say "I quit. I can't work with these people."

As he explored his assessments, he saw that expecting people to whom he made requests to know what he is asking and why, and to fulfill his request accordingly may be reasonable in the army, but may not be as reasonable in a civilian setting. He could see that in the military, people undergo similar training, share a similar background, and are expected to fulfill orders made by their superiors. In civilian settings people often do not share similar training. They come from different backgrounds and professions, and may not understand what you are asking them to do or why. They may, in good faith, attempt to do what they think you are asking, but their interpretation may be different than yours or they may have a different order of priorities. Civilians don't have ranks and may not feel compelled to do something just because someone asks them to. Before they commit to doing something, they may need to understand why it is important.

As Mike explored the assessments behind his moods with his team, he began to see actions that he could take to develop his capacity to make requests more effectively in a civilian setting. He made an assessment to the team member who had not stayed close: "I was a bit frustrated that you did not stay as close as I asked." The team member responded: "I stayed close. I was listening to the conversation. I just went a few feet ahead to see what we might be facing so that I could tell the team."

Reflecting on his team member's response, Mike realized that sometimes people did not do what he asked simply because they did not understand what he wanted or why he wanted it, not because they were incompetent or not interested in working with him. He realized the importance of two key elements of a request: 1) taking time to discuss the conditions of fulfillment when making a request—what do you want done and how? and 2) building a background of obviousness to ensure that the people listening have more background for understanding his request. In this case, Mike's team did not have any idea why he made the request that they stay close, and as a result, one team member who thought he was fulfilling Mike's request did exactly what Mike was trying to avoid. Upon reflection, Mike realized that his request could have been more effective if he had not just given an order to stay close, but also shared the assessments he was making that led him to make that request. He could have said something like: "There are lots of enemies here, and if we get too close to them, they will attack us. It is important to stay close and not to move so we don't accidentally attract them to us. Is everybody okay with this?"

Upon reflecting on this situation and others like it, Mike realized that the moods of frustration, resignation and distrust that he often found himself in were not conducive to working with civilians, or to learning to lead and collaborate in a civilian setting. By exploring the assessments behind these moods, Mike realized that he simply did not know how to make requests in a way that would produce the results he was looking for, and began to see how to make his requests more effective. He resolved to take action to build a shared understanding, and to share the concerns he was attempting to address. He also discovered that sometimes his team members did not accept his requests because they felt they had a better or different way of accomplishing the same objectives. His assessment that they did not want to fulfill his requests because they were either incompetent or not interested in collaborating to complete the missions was unfounded. Rather than give up on working with them, he resolved to keep making requests, but also resolved to share the assessments he had that led to his requests. They could all explore them together, and be on the same page as to what they should do to increase their likelihood of success. By exploring his moods and the underlying assessments triggering them, Mike was able to shift moods that were not conducive to learning to make effective requests in a civilian setting to moods of resolution and commitment. He resolved to build trust with his team, and to not give up.

Learning to Make Effective Offers

The other conversational move we can make to get something done is to make an offer: a conditional promise to take care of something that the listener is concerned about if the listener accepts our offer. During the course, participants also read about offers and are introduced to the essential elements of an offer:[46]

1. Speaker
2. Listener
3. Conditions of Fulfillment
4. Background of Obviousness
5. Offer/Promise: Action to be performed in the future by person making the offer/promise.
6. Specified time for fulfillment of the offer

As with requests, on paper this seems simple enough. However, in our experience working with people in the WEST course, people often don't make offers, even when it would be of great benefit to the team if they did. Alternatively, they make offers, but their offers are not accepted or they don't produce the desired result. Consequently, not only are there missed opportunities that could add value to our teams, but also team members find themselves in negative moods that are not conducive to continued collaboration and to achieving their goals.

---

46 See Flores, *Conversations for Action and Collected Essays*, 10.

➤   Case Study #8: Learning to make offers

"It is not okay to make offers. It is presumptuous to assume that I know something that my colleagues don't."

(From resignation about making offers to resolving to learn to make offers.)

Chris, a senior consultant and project manager at a global energy company, was placed in a team with people he had never met from the United States, Australia, and Mexico. During the team exercises, Chris was very quiet. He hardly spoke unless someone asked him a question. A couple of weeks into the course, I read his written responses to a homework assignment that showed that he had a lot to say about the work that he and his team had been doing, none of which he had discussed with his team. We scheduled a one-on-one conversation, and when we spoke, it became apparent that Chris had many interesting observations about how the team was working together, including what he thought was working well and what was not working so well. He had very good suggestions about new practices that could help the team. However, he was very reluctant to bring these to them. "Who am I to impose my ideas on them? They are smart people. What they eventually come up with is just as good, if not better, than what I come up with." I encouraged him to make proposals to his team, but not much changed in the next exercise. I asked him about it, and he just did not think it was appropriate to tell his team what he thought they should do. He was in a mood of resignation about making offers. He felt that move was not possible for him. Shortly thereafter, his own team members began to tell him that they felt that he was holding back, and that from reading his homework assignments, they knew that he had more to offer and they wondered why he didn't speak up.

As he reflected on this, Chris began to see that not only during the team exercises, but in life, he seldom made offers, which was a stumbling block for him because he wanted to become an entrepreneur. "How am I going to sell my services if I can't bring myself to offer them to people?" Chris was a very bright man, whose performance people often complimented. He was very comfortable accepting requests from his bosses or from his colleagues, but he was uncomfortable making offers. He did not want to be seen as presump-tuous or to act like he knew more than others. "Ever since I was little, I was taught not to be presumptuous and not to assume that I know more than oth-ers." As a result, there were many opportunities that passed him by, and he did not pursue opportunities that could be interesting to him and/or others. Making an offer was simply something that he could not do, even though he could see that it was important if he was going to succeed as an entrepreneur.

By reflecting on his experiences with his teams during the course, Chris be-gan to see that an offer was really an opportunity to take care of someone else's concern. If the recipient of an offer judges that the offer is valuable because it addresses something she cares about, then she is likely to accept it. Otherwise, she will say no. His assessment that making an offer was not appropriate because it was presumptuous changed. If he was able to ad-dress people's concerns, people would find that valuable, not presumptuous and immodest. Since he could see the importance of learning to make offers if he was going to take on more entrepreneurial projects, Chris resolved to get better at making offers and to begin practicing making more of them, something that was very uncomfortable for him. During his team exercises, he made offers to lead, to research certain aspects of the game, to help team-mates when he thought they needed help, and so on. He began to practice doing this outside the course as well. Since the class ended, he has offered to organize a large family reunion and is indeed pursuing various entrepre-neurial ventures.

➤ Case Study #9: Learning to make effective offers
"I made an offer that people seem to like but nothing happened."

(From frustration, resignation, and distrust to resolution.)

Jane, a navy reservist and avid *World of Warcraft* player in real-life, was placed in a team with people who did not have much, if any, video game experience. She was concerned about the team's ability to successfully complete the assigned *World of Warcraft* missions given their lack of competence in the game. She reached out to Mary, the team member who had agreed to play the role of tank, a very important role on a *World of Warcraft* team. Mary was probably the person on the team who had the least experience in the game, and the one who felt most anxious about letting the team down. Jane offered to spend time with Mary in the game and to train her as a tank. Mary said, "That would be great. Thank you so much!" The time for their next scheduled team exercise arrived, and the team failed. Jane and Mary had not met prior to the meeting, and it was clear that Mary still did not know how to perform her role as tank.

Jane found herself in the following moods:

Frustration: She wanted to complete the mission successfully, but her team's lack of skill made it impossible.

Resignation: She did not see that there was anything that they could do to complete the mission, or anything that she could do to help them, despite being an expert in *World of Warcraft*. "It would have been nice if Mary had practiced her tank. If she doesn't know what to do, we will continue to fail."

Distrust: She made offers to Mary and others to help them become more competent in their roles, but even though Mary said yes, it did not happen.

During the debrief, Jane said that she was disappointed that they had not been able to complete the mission, and then proceeded to say, "I wish Mary had had a chance to practice her tank."

"Did you make her an offer to train her?" I asked.

"Yes."

"What happened?"

"She said yes, but I guess she couldn't meet. She must have been busy."

At that point I asked her if they had ever committed to a time to meet, and Jane said they had not. Upon further discussion, she began to see that a fundamental element of an offer is a specified time for fulfillment of the offer, and the importance of both sides reaching agreement about that. Mary's response to Jane's offer – "That would be great" – was not a promise to meet with Jane at a particular time so that she could get better at playing her role as tank. It was the equivalent of "That's a great idea." As Jane realized that, she saw something that she could do to make a more effective offer next time, and her mood of resignation began to shift. Instead of dwelling in resignation, Jane saw action that she could take to help the team complete the game objectives and resolved to make another offer to meet, but this time she asked Mary to agree to a specific time. She and Mary met, and Mary began to learn how to perform the tank role for the team.

Learning to Negotiate, Including Counteroffering and Saying "No"
In order for action to occur between two people, one person must make a request or an offer to get things started. As we saw above, although those moves seem simple, many of us don't feel comfortable making them, or we make them in an ineffective manner. We fail to get the result that we want.

Once a request or an offer is made, a response is necessary from the listener in order to keep the cycle of coordination moving forward. "We only can produce action together if we have a mutual commitment from both the customer and the performer."[47] After a request or an offer is made, a process of negotiation may ensue. Possible responses include a commitment to commit later, an acceptance, a counteroffer, or a decline. If one of these moves is not made, the cycle of coordination is broken and it can get in the way of the team's ability to collaborate. During the WEST course, participants have plenty of occasions to make Requests and/or Offers to their team members, and it is not unusual for someone to not get a response. Instead of an acceptance, they simply get ignored, leading the person making the request or the offer to make assumptions about the silence and to fall into bad moods that are not conducive to collaborating with the rest of the team. For example:

- Distrust: "I made a request via e-mail, but no one responded. I guess they are not interested in what I am doing. They don't care about it."
- Resignation: "I made an offer, but no one responded. I have made many offers before that I think would be beneficial to our group, but they seem to fall on deaf ears. No one responds. There is no point in continuing to try."
- Resentment: "Everyone says they want to be successful, but when I request a meeting to see how we are doing, no one responds to my request. We continue to run around, doing our own thing, not talking with each other, and as a result we are going to fail. When I try to do

---

47 See Flores, *Conversations for Action and Collected Essays*, 8.

something about it, I get ignored. Because of them, we are all going to fail."

By becoming aware of moods, and by learning to explore them, participants in the WEST course become very aware of the importance of responding to offers and/or requests, even if they don't accept them. They realize that once a request or an offer is made, the ball is in the listener's court to respond. Ignoring our colleagues could lead to a deterioration of the team's ability to work together because it can negatively impact their mood, as well as the morale of the team as a whole. A response, however, does not mean having to say yes.

In our experience we find that many people say yes when they really want to say no or when they really should make a counteroffer instead. Saying yes in situations where it would be more appropriate to say no or to counteroffer can also hinder collaboration and effective work in teams.

If we don't say no to a request that we can't fulfill, we may be causing harm to a person who is counting on us to deliver something and who is no longer looking for an alternative because they trust us to do it. If we don't say no or make a counteroffer to a request that we can fulfill but that will put other commitments in jeopardy, others may be disappointed and we may fall into a mood of overwhelm. If we say yes to an offer that we don't find valuable, the person who made the offer may wind up doing a lot of work for something that is not appreciated. Distrust can grow. "I fulfilled my promise, but my work is not recognized. I wish they had not said yes. I wasted my time doing work that no one appreciates."

Why don't we say no? Why don't we counteroffer? In our experience, often people don't feel comfortable making these moves. They have the assessment that saying no is inappropriate:

- They think saying no to someone will offend them. Saying no is rejecting someone. It is not nice to reject people.

- They think if they say no, people will think they are not a committed team player.
- They think if they don't say yes, people will judge them as not valuable to the team or accuse them of not being a team player.

Consequently, even when the best thing for them (and for their team) would be to say no, or to counteroffer, they are in a mood of resignation with respect to their ability to do so. Those moves are simply not available to them. They feel that their only choice is to say yes. Learning to make those moves is an important part of learning to coordinate our commitments and to work effectively in teams.

➤ Case Study #10: Learning to say 'No'
"I can't say no to my team. Saying no would make me show up as uncommitted to my team."

(From distrust, resignation, and overwhelm to trust.)

Beth, a senior consultant to technology companies, signed up for the WEST course on a friend's recommendation, and the two friends decided to participate on the same team. She did not have any particular learning goals, but she hoped to learn something new that could help her work more effectively, because she often felt stretched thin and overwhelmed. She was very busy, but felt she could dedicate a few hours a week to playing *World of Warcraft*, which we confirmed would be enough to adequately participate in the course.

Towards the end of the course, we asked her team to acquire a horse, which meant that some of the participants would have to increase two or three levels to be able to get to level 20, the level the game required a player to attain to get a horse. Beth and her teammates were level 18. We offered everyone who was at level 18 or below assistance, and gave them the option of letting us level up their avatar for them so that they would not have to spend extra time playing. Beth's teammates expressed a desire to level up their avatars together so that they could continue to practice together and learn their avatars' new capabilities as they reached higher levels. Beth did not have any time to play with them as she was leaving for Europe the next day and had important presentations to make to her clients while there. She told her team that she could not meet with them at any of the times they proposed, but agreed to level up her avatar by herself. She did not accept our offer to do that work for her.

Beth left on her trip, and the morning after her arrival, she got up at dawn to spend a couple of hours leveling up to get "the goddamn horse." When she told me about that a couple of days later, she was upset with me for telling her that she had to spend less time playing the game than she actually did. She felt that I had misled her. I asked her why she had not accepted our offer to level up her avatar, because if she had, she certainly would not have had to spend hours leveling up her avatar to get the horse. I told her that we were mindful of people's time and were sincere in our offer to do that work for them so that they would not have to spend additional time in the game. Accepting our offer, I told her, was a valid way of fulfilling our requirements for the next team exercise. "My team thought it was important that we all level our avatars up together," she said. I pointed out that she was unable to do that work with them, and as such, she did the leveling up all by herself. "Well, they thought it was important that we continue to practice with our avatars so that we could learn any new powers or spells that we get as we level up. I could not say no because I did not want to be the one that showed up as uncommitted."

Upon reflection, Beth acknowledged that while talking about the horse with her team, she wanted to say no to their request that she level up her avatar by herself so that she continue learning her avatar's capabilities. Her schedule was packed and she did not have time to level up her avatar. Yet she could not bring herself to say no. Beth identified two moods that blocked her:

Distrust: Beth felt that if she said no, her teammates would not empathize with all the other commitments she had on her plate that week, and despite her crazy travel schedule and client commitments, they would still think that she was uncommitted to the team if she did not do what they thought was important.

Resignation: Since the team thought it was important for everyone to level up his or her own avatar, she had to do it as well. There was nothing else that she could do, otherwise they would assess her as uncommitted, and she did not want them to judge her that way.

By exploring her assessments, Beth began to see that they were not well grounded. She saw that she could have accepted our offer, and still taken care of her team members' concern that she learn her avatar's new powers and spells. She did not have to do the leveling up on her own to learn new powers and spells. She could have asked our team to spend 15 to 20 minutes with her to train her and she could have practiced with her avatar once it was already at a higher level.

She also saw that by trying to prove that she was committed to her team, she fell into moods of frustration and overwhelm. "Even though I know I should not have given myself additional work last week because my agenda was absolutely full, I still ended up making new promises and committing hours of my time that I did not have." She could have asked for our assistance, but she did not think that it was appropriate for her to do so given her teammates' desires. Ironically, by trying to prove that she was committed, she found herself not wanting to participate with her team any longer. By wanting the team to trust her, she fell into distrust. She was busy, and if they were going to require so much of her, then she could not do it. She thought about quitting her team and the course.

Beth realized that saying no is appropriate and necessary at times, and it does not mean that you are not committed to the team. In fact, it can sometimes be the best move to build trust and to maintain a committed and engaged team. As a result of this experience, Beth reported being more open to saying no to people. Learning to say no more often would require practice, because it was not comfortable for her, but at least now, she saw the benefit of being open to learning to do so.

DEVELOPING OUR ABILITY TO MAKE, LISTEN TO, AND EXPLORE ASSESSMENTS

A Brief Note on Assessments

As mentioned earlier, as human beings we constantly make and operate with assessments. This is how we evaluate what is going on around us, and how we determine what actions to take to accomplish something we care about. For example, when working on a team, we might have an assessment that something is missing or broken, and as a result, we could make an offer or a request to someone to take care of what we think is missing or not working. If we have an assessment that roles are unclear in our team, that is an opportunity to make a request to have a conversation where roles could be clarified, or to declare new roles, and hence enable team members to assume new responsibilities and coordinate more effectively. If we make the assessment that different team members have different interpretations of the team's mission, it is an opportunity to explore the various interpretations and together declare a mission that is shared by all team members. If we make an assessment that people have a different standard of performance, it is an opportunity to articulate and declare a new standard that all will commit to sharing. This sounds simple enough. But in real life, although we make assessments all the time, it can be difficult to make our assessments public and directly to someone else and to listen to assessments others make about us. We get nervous. We feel afraid. We feel physically uncomfortable. Not surprisingly, we often don't tell each other what we think. We have habits that prevent us from making assessments, and we have habits that keep us from listening to them.

When it comes to engaging in conversations where we could explore each other's assessments, the following often occurs instead:

- We have assessments but we don't make them public. We keep them private. We have assessments that get in the way of making assessments. For example, we think that it is not polite to say something negative. We think that it is not appropriate to say something that may be critical. We think others will take offense. We think that our assessments may not be important.
- We don't listen to someone else's assessment. Rather than asking questions about the assessment and what the person wants to achieve by making the assessment, we dismiss it or get defensive. If it is an assessment that we interpret as complimentary to us, we may dismiss it as unimportant. If it is an assessment that we interpret as critical to us, we may feel like we are being attacked. We give explanations instead of asking questions to explore why the person made the assessment in the first place.
- We shut down the conversation before it even begins.

If we don't share our assessments, we miss opportunities to improve our work or invent something new together; we unintentionally allow moods of resignation and distrust to fester in the background, and we diminish our team's ability to invent new ways to work together to complete our mission. But if we are able to develop our ability to make and listen to assessments, we find that the reciprocal nature of giving and receiving assessments creates intimacy, builds trust, and changes the mood of teams.

In order to work effectively with others, it is critical that we build our capacity to make and receive assessments, and we can only build this capacity through practice. The more we practice, the less trapped we become in our historical patterns and areas of blindness. The more we practice, the less likely we are to remain hostages to unproductive moods. The more we practice, the more new opportunities emerge for designing our futures with other people, including people who may see the world very differently than the way that we see it.

As with requests and offers, participants in the course are introduced to assessments as a new distinction for the effective coordination of action. This is not because they are not already making assessments in their real lives, but because we have found that most of us have not been taught to engage in these conversations in very productive ways, ways that open possibilities for new actions, instead of shutting them down. In learning to listen to assessments and to explore them with our teammates, we may have to unlearn habits that get in the way of listening. We may, for example, have to get rid of our automatic assessment that we are being attacked when we receive something that we think is critical of our performance, which leads us to fall into a defensive mood where listening is not possible.

The fundamental elements of an assessment are:

1) Speaker
2) Listener
3) Making a verdict
4) Can be grounded or ungrounded. There is or there isn't evidence that supports it. It is not a fact. It is never true or false.
5) For grounding:
   a. For the sake of what are you making this assessment? What domain of concern are you addressing? What would you like to happen in the future?
   b. Hypothesis of recurrence. Is there a pattern of facts that supports it?
   c. Standards upon which you base your verdict.

Again, these elements seem easy enough to understand and apply, but in reality, it takes practice and reflection. We need to begin to embody these elements and to develop the ability to make and receive assessments for the sake of inventing new actions we want to take together. During the WEST course, people become aware that:

- Often people don't make explicit the assessments that they have. There is no speaker. A person may find herself frustrated about a situation. She may, for example, have the assessment that something should be happening that is not or that the team is doing something that they should not be doing. But even though she has these assessments, she does not make them public to her team. Consequently, the team is deprived of a conversation that could have led them to take new actions that would have been helpful.

- For assessments to be effective, they need to be directed at a listener, but often there isn't anyone in that position. Instead, people regularly make general assessments. *It would be good if we all knew our roles. It would be nice if we were prepared.* But if we don't engage in direct conversations with people, we are unlikely to make commitments to take care of the concerns behind our assessments. In the course, team members must become competent in their roles so that they can accomplish the mission. If someone does not know how to perform their role, or is not doing something that someone else thinks they should be able to do, it is important that other members of the team make an assessment to that they can get on the same page about action that they could take. For example, a teammate could make a request that the person gets training and the person whose performance is not up to par yet can promise to get training. If assessments are not made directly, effective action is unlikely to follow.

- Other times, people state a number of facts but don't make an assessment: "Rose was late. Two of us had not read the homework. Bob was not at the level required." In this example, the person really had the following assessments but did not make them: "As a team, we are not committed to fulfilling the mission. Rose arriving late gives us less time and that does not work. Not reading the homework prior to our meeting forced us to spend time on getting up to speed, which gave us less time to actually complete the mission. Bob not being at the required level made us spend extra time doing something that was required for us to obtain the mission, again giving us less time. If we don't commit to fixing these problems, we are going to have the same outcome next time. I think it is important that we succeed in the missions that we are assigned." By making this type of assessment, the person can proceed to take actions, like making a request to Rose to be on time next time, or a request to the team that everybody read the homework assignment prior to the meeting, or an offer to help the team prepare by sending a reminder of the required levels prior to team meetings, and so forth.

Throughout the course, participants have many opportunities to make assessments to each other, to notice when some of the elements of an assessment are missing, and to explore assessments with each other. During the first few weeks, we treat participants in the course like beginners in learning to make and explore assessments. We introduce them to the fundamental elements of an assessment. We give them a script to practice having conversations with each other. It's very mechanical, but our focus is on reminding them why these conversations are important, and on encouraging them to make assessments and explore them together to see what happens. As the course progresses, they no longer use a script, but they continue to practice every week with each other. In every team exercise, they share their assessments about what worked, what did not work, how well they feel they performed, how well their team-mates performed, and so forth. Conversations are a bit awkward at first, and we have to encourage them to make assessments and to ask questions about them, but by the end of the course, participants make many assessments that lead to something useful for a specific team member or for the team as a whole. They are less focused on making sure they cover all of the elements of an assessment, and more oriented to supporting each other to produce the results they want to produce together. One important contribution of the game to their learning regarding how they make and listen to assessments is that they can see how the assessments they make and the actions that they subsequently commit to help them produce better results, which reinforces their learning. "That worked! Let me try it again!" Participants begin to experience assessments not as personal attacks, but rather as conversations that open up a space of exploration where they can learn about each other's concerns, and see what actions they can take to address them if necessary.

➤ Case Study #11: Learning to listen to assessments as an opportunity for action, not as a criticism.

"You are not good at navigating."

Embarrassed: "I know. I am sorry."

(From confusion, embarrassment, and frustration to confidence in the team and trust.)

Sue, a consultant who had never played video games before, found herself constantly getting lost in the game. She was a bit embarrassed, and no matter how hard she tried to stay close to her teammates' avatars in the game, she often got lost and the team would spend five to 10 minutes trying to find her. Their attempts to find her were often made more difficult because Sue tended not to call out when she was lost. Instead of speaking up, she would suffer in silence while she desperately tried to figure out on her own how to get back to the team. When she did speak up, her voice revealed her frustration. She did not want to get lost, but she often did, no matter how hard she tried to keep up with the team. She felt that finding her way around was something that she should be able to do – all of her teammates were together after all – but she could not. She felt guilty because she thought that she was holding the team back, and thought that if only she was better at directions, she would not do so. This was not an enjoyable experience for her. She wondered why she had signed up for the course. When we began the part of the course where we encourage team members to make direct assessments to each other, one of her team mates told her: "Sue, you are not good with directions and that makes the rest of the team waste too much time looking for you." When she first heard this assessment from her teammate, Sue felt embarrassed and simply agreed with him. "You are right. I am not good with directions. This is very frustrating for me."

But, with some encouragement from us, she continued to explore the assessment:

"Why do you see my getting lost as a waste of the team's time?"

"We have limited time to complete our missions and we usually have to spend at least 10 minutes finding you so that we can complete our assignments together."

"Do you have any recommendations for me?"

"You can learn to read the map in the game and ask us how to get to where we are going. I can show you how to use the map."

"Okay, thank you! I accept, but in real life, I am not that great with maps and I am afraid I will continue to hold back the team."

"Well, why don't you just stick close to me in the game. I will keep an eye on you. If you don't see me, tell me right away."

"Okay."

Then another team member chimed in:

"You know, there is a function in the game that allows you to follow someone automatically. Let me show you how you can follow Rob."

"Great! Thank you!"

"And I will travel behind you guys in case something happens. I will keep an eye on you too and make sure that we stay together as a team."

"Thank you."

As a result of this conversation, the team adopted a new practice for traveling that enabled them to reach their destinations quicker. Hence what Sue had originally heard as a judgment of her became a conversation about what the team could do to travel faster given Sue's current navigational skills. As a result, offers and requests were made, and a new team practice was implemented. After this exercise, Sue reflected on her mood and stated that she was much more confident in her team's ability to succeed in the future, and that she felt trust towards her teammates and their desire to help her.

➤ Case Study #12: Opening new possibilities with customers by learning to explore complaints as assessments

"I go the extra mile for my clients. I do more than our contract requires me to do. Yet they still complain. I try to avoid my clients."

(From defensiveness and distrust to trust and collaboration.)

Jim, an owner of a commercial real estate management company, observed that he felt very uncomfortable receiving assessments from his teammates during the course. Even though the assessments he received had to do with how he led the team during an exercise in *World of Warcraft*, he noticed that he was not comfortable, and that rather than asking his teammates more questions about the assessments, as we had encouraged participants to do to see if they could see actions that they could take in the future together, Jim fell into a mood of defensiveness. Not only did he not agree with his teammate's assessments, but he also felt like his teammate was attacking him, and that he had to defend himself from the attack. By stepping back and exploring that assessment, Jim was able to see that his teammate had no intention of attacking him, and that he was merely pointing out that he felt lost at certain points during Jim's leadership and that in the future he would find it helpful if Jim checked in a bit more with him to make sure that he knew what they were doing and what his role was. Once they agreed to that, a simple practice of asking him, "Do you have any questions or are you ready to go?" went a long way for that teammate.

Jim found the exercises with his team interesting and was surprised by the level of trust they seemed to have cultivated in a short time, but he was skeptical about the possibility of engaging in this type of conversation with his clients in real life. When I explored this issue with Jim later, he told me: "In the game, we can build trust because you guys are here and we are all learning together, but in real life it is different. I hate it when my customers call with complaints about the work that my company does for them. I am a very hard worker and do everything that is contractually required and more; yet they still call to complain. I find myself getting defensive, and even though I prove that I am doing everything that the contract requires, they are still not happy. I would rather not talk with them!"

In the conversation, however, Jim saw that his customers' complaints were simply assessments, not attacks on his character, and that if he learned to explore them, he could learn a lot about his customers' concerns, and perhaps make new offers to them to take care of those concerns. He saw the conversations as an opportunity to build trust with his customers instead of as something to avoid. He began to practice approaching complaints as assessments with his clients and found that he had much better results. He went from dreading those conversations to looking forward to them, and was very pleased when a client that he had found difficult before told him that he was doing a great job and that he looked forward to continuing to work with him.

➤ Case Study #13: Making new offers as a result of learning to explore assessments
"We went from the worst month of the year in sales to the best month of the year within weeks."

(From defensiveness and distrust to perplexity and resolution.)

Marco, VP of Sales of a household goods company, signed up for the WEST course because he was confident that the skills we focus on were relevant to him and the teams that he manages, particularly the skill of listening. He shared that some of the people who report to him do not always listen to him and that they often want to do things their own way despite what he wants them to do. "Listening is very important," he said, "but sometimes, I don't know how to get a colleague to listen to me."

Four or five weeks into the course, during a team exercise in *World of Warcraft* in which Marco was the designated leader, he experienced a situation with some of his teammates that was similar to what he had been experiencing in real life. As leader, Marco spent time prior to the exercise preparing: He read the assignment carefully; he did most of the assignment with a practice avatar; and he came up with a strategy for the team to follow. When they met to do the exercise as a team, Marco gave them instructions, including which path to take to get to one of their destinations. On that point, one of his teammates, Sean, said he did not think that was the best way to go. "I think we should go down to the river and walk alongside it to our destination. It is safer." In a slightly irritated tone, Marco said: "Fine. If you want to go that way, we can."

After the exercise was over, Marco said during the debrief, "It is interesting to me how hard it is for people to accept that someone else is the leader and that they have to listen to that person." When asked to elaborate, Marco said, "The team agreed that I would be the leader this week. I spent time researching this exercise and preparing for it. I came up with a strategy that I wanted to implement, but Sean still wanted to do something different. He did not accept my leadership."

"Why do you have the assessment that he did not accept your leadership?" I asked him.

"Well, he did not want to go the direction that I asked them to go and suggested a different path," he said.

"I am not sure if that is questioning your leadership. He had a different assessment than you about which path to take. He had the assessment that walking along the river in this part of the game was safer because there are fewer computer-generated enemies there. He had the assessment that the path that you asked them to take was less safe because it would expose you to more computer-generated enemies and you would come under attack more often," I said. "Is that questioning your leadership or is that simply making an assessment for the sake of helping the team get to your destination in a safer way?" Listening to the conversation, Sean commented that his intention was the latter. He said he would have been fine if Marco did not accept his recommendation.

Reflecting on this question and on the experience in general, Marco could see that he had fallen into a mood of defensiveness that prevented him from listening to and exploring his teammates' assessments. He was in a mood of distrust towards Sean and assumed that Sean did not trust him either, given that he contradicted his orders. He thought that Sean did not listen to him and undermined his leadership. He also saw that the mood of defensiveness and distrust did not allow him to be open to listening to Sean and to asking him questions about his assessments, including questions like, "Why do you think it is safer to go down to the river?" or "Why do you think the way I am asking you guys to take is more dangerous?" By exploring the assessment, he realized, he and the rest of the team could learn more about the mechanics of the game from Sean, who seemed to know a bit more about it, and as a leader, Marco could decide to adopt the recommendation or to decline. If he still wanted to go on the route he proposed for some other reason, possibly to give the team the opportunity to practice fighting together, he could respond by articulating that reason. As a result of this conversation, Marco also saw how cultivating a mood of perplexity about other people's assessments could help him to: ask more questions about the assessments of others that could lead to new actions that he had not contemplated before; and improve his own listening by helping him to shift out of a mood of defensiveness that is not conducive to asking questions.

Days after the exercise, Marco continued to reflect on how often he mistook assessments as assertions, and failed to explore them. One that was particularly perplexing to him was an assessment at work that he and everybody else in his company had treated like a fact for many years: "December is the worst month for sales." Consequently, sales people did not make much effort to sell in December. Marco, who was now the VP of Sales for the company, agreed that the month of December had in fact been a poor month for sales for many years, but he wondered if that had to continue to be the case. "We sell household goods. You would think that people would want to buy these during the holidays to give as presents, or to use themselves." He realized that the claim that "December is a bad month for sales" was just an assessment that they had treated as an assertion, a fact, which put them in a mood of resignation about it. There was no point in doing anything different to increase sales in December because December was a bad month for sales. Marco did not understand why

December should be a bad month, and by treating "December is a bad month for sales" as an assessment, Marco resolved to explore what actions he and the company could take to improve December sales.

He talked to sales people and asked questions about what kept people from buying in December, and he talked to his CFO to see what offers they could make to help people with cash-flow constraints. Working closely with him and the CEO, they made new offers to potential customers. As a result, not only was that December the best December ever, but it was also the best month of the entire year.

➤ Case Study #14: Learning to listen and to explore assessments
"No We Can't."

"Yes We Can."

(From resignation, impatience, arrogance, and distrust to resolving to explore assessments for the sake of learning and helping the team work more effectively together.)

Larry, a professor of engineering, and Jose, a software developer, were assigned to a team that also included a Navy officer, a non-profit executive, and a college professor on leadership. In one of their assignments, we asked that they complete a mission and recommended a route to them. Unbeknownst to most of the team, the route we recommended – which in our opinion was the best route for them to take – was broken and it would probably require them to jump, which many of them had not done before. A comedy of errors ensued as follows:

- Jose designated himself team leader for this part of the mission.
- The team got to the point where the road was broken and they had to figure out how to pass to the other side. Had they jumped, they would have made it, but four out of the five team members did not know jumping was a possibility.

- Larry, who had taken this course once before, knew that jumping was possible. He had completed this exercise before with a prior team.
- Cindy, one of their team members, fell off on the wrong side of the wall and her avatar quickly came under attack and died. Jose told her to come back, and after struggling to do it by herself for a while, she somehow made her way back, but immediately made the same mistake again. Jose told her to "Jump right," and a frustrated Cindy said, "If I knew how, I would." Cindy fell quiet and once again struggled to make her way back to the team on her own.

In the meantime, the rest of the team tried to figure out what to do. Should they jump? Should they find an alternative route?

Larry: "I think we have to jump here."

Jose: "We cannot jump."

Larry: "I think we can jump here."

Jose: With a tone of impatience and irritation, "We absolutely cannot jump here. We have to go back to where we came from and go the other route."

Larry: "Okay, but I think we can."

Jose: "I hate jumping. I quit playing videogames because I hate jumping. We can't jump. Let's go."

Without noticing that Larry had "accidentally fallen" in the direction that they were supposed to go a couple of times without dying right away,[48] the team followed Jose's direction, leaving Cindy to fend for herself and to reunite later once she was able to find the team on her own. They wasted a lot of time, got separated from each other, took the longer route to their destination, and

---

48 His avatar died shortly thereafter since he was alone in enemy territory and he was attacked by computer-generated enemies of higher levels that he could not fend off by himself.

came under many attacks from higher level critters, attacks that they would not have had to endure had they gone the route we recommended they take. In the end, they did not accomplish the assigned mission.

Why did the mission unfold this way? Mainly because:

1) Jose confused assessments with assertions,
2) Jose did not explore Larry's assessment, and
3) Larry simply fell into a mood of resignation about his ability to be heard by his teammates and gave up.

During the debrief, Jose reported: "I am frustrated. I wanted to complete the mission, but we got separated as a team. Everyone has different abilities and we wasted time discussing stuff that did not need to be discussed. We should not have spent time discussing whether or not to jump because I knew that it was not possible."

"Are you sure?" I asked him.

"Yes," he said. "I tried it with an alternative avatar earlier, and I died a bunch of times."

"Is it possible that you don't know how to jump, and perhaps you could learn?" I asked.

"I definitely don't know how to jump," he responded.

"Did you notice that Larry kept saying that he thought you guys had to jump and that you guys could jump?"

Jose: "But I was pretty sure that I could not."

Me: "Yes, but that is an assessment based on your experience. It is not a fact. Thus far, you have not been able to jump and so you thought that it was not possible. Larry, you may remember, is reviewing this course, and chances are that he has done this exercise before. Perhaps it would make sense to pause and ask him why he thinks that you guys can jump to see if there is something new to learn. Larry, do you know whether or not you can jump here?"

Larry: "Yes. You can jump. I have done it before. In fact, I did this exact same exercise some time ago. And when I said that we could jump, I was saying it from the ground as I accidentally fell, and my avatar survived the fall."

Me: "Why did you not say that, Larry?"

Larry: "I don't know. I think I fell into a mood of resignation. Jose kept insisting that it could not be done, and I thought that maybe the team can't jump here, and decided to go along with whatever Jose said at that moment. He seemed impatient and ready to go, and so I gave up. I am frustrated with myself."

Learning for Jose:
Jose confused an assessment with an assertion. Jose asserted that jumping was not possible with absolute certainty, when in reality the situation was that he did not know how to jump, and that he did not know what could be done differently at that moment. If he had been open to listening to Larry's assessments, Jose would have learned that they could, in fact, jump.

Two moods prevented Jose from listening to Larry's assessment at that moment:

> Arrogance: Jose thought he knew all there was to know about the situation. His assessment was right or a fact, and it was not important for him to listen to Larry since he was obviously wrong. As you may remember from the first part of this book, the mood of arrogance is one that often gets in the way of learning anything new. Not surprisingly, it also gets in the way of listening.

Impatience: He had the assessment that the conversation about whether or not you could jump was irrelevant because he already knew that it could not be done, and that they just needed to get going and not talk about it. Asking Larry why he thought they could jump seemed a waste of time to Jose, since he was convinced that he was right.

This experience, and the guided reflection afterwards, made Jose realize the importance of distinguishing an assessment – an automatic evaluation of the situation based on our experience – from an assertion, a statement of fact. Jose realized that although his statement that they could not jump was only an assessment based on his experience with jumping, he treated it as if it were a fact, and by doing so, he was not disposed to listening to and exploring Larry's assessment. He simply thought Larry was wrong. He saw that if he had taken the time to explore Larry's assessment, the team would have benefited in various ways: learning to jump, not getting dispersed, and successfully completing the mission in the time allotted. Reflecting on his real life, Jose observed that he often falls into moods of impatience and arrogance, and he wondered how many opportunities he may be missing out on by not listening to other assessments and by treating his own assessments like facts. To further develop his ability to listen, he began to practice:

1) Distinguishing assessments from assertions;
2) Pausing to observe and reflect on the moods that he found himself in, and paying particular attention when he found himself in moods of impatience or arrogance, since he could see how these moods negatively impact his ability to listen; and
3) Cultivating a mood of patience by pausing more to explore other people's assessments even if he does not agree with them.

Learning for Larry

The week prior to this exercise, Larry had an assessment that he did not share with the team, and had he done so, the team would likely have been much more successful than they were. As a result of that exercise, Larry was resolved to contribute to the team's success and to articulate whatever assessments he had that he thought could be important. His moment came when they got to the part of the road that was broken.

Given that he was reviewing this course and had previously done the same exercise with another team, he knew for a fact that jumping was possible and survivable, and his assessment was that the team should jump. He told his team that they could and should jump, a couple of times, but they didn't listen. When Jose contradicted him and told the team to go the other way, Larry gave up.

During the debrief session, Larry said that he was frustrated and resigned. In particular, he felt frustrated because he wanted to contribute to the team, but was unable to do so. He was sure that if his team had listened to his assessment, they would have had a better outcome. He felt resigned about his ability to make assessments effectively:

"I understand that assessments are important, but I can't seem to make them in a manner that produces what I want to produce. Last week I didn't make an assessment. Consequently, we were not successful as a team. I was resolved to practice making assessments this week, and I did, but my team members did not listen to me."

He was beginning to think that this was an important distinction on paper, but one that didn't produce much for him in real life.

Larry was in a mood of resignation and thought that there was nothing he could have done that would have led his team members to listen to his assessment. However, as we explored the issues surrounding assessments together, like why we make assessments and what are the fundamental elements of an assessment, Larry began to see that he could have shared more with his team, which might have helped them see why he was making the assessment and what he wanted to accomplish as a result. It was not enough to say, "You can and should jump," especially if someone else had a different interpretation. He saw that he could have provided more evidence to ground his assessment that would have allowed the team to see why he thought they should jump. In this case, he saw that he could have said something like:

"I think we should jump. I have done this exercise before and know that it is okay to jump. Also, today I accidentally fell and survived the fall. I am confident that we can jump. I think we should jump because it is the recommended path and I know the other side has enemies that are at a much higher level than we are."

Members of his team, including Jose, agreed that had Larry made his assessment this way, they would have listened to him and followed his advice. Consequently, Larry felt ambitious about learning to make assessments more effectively and resolved to continue to practice. The mood of resignation that he had fallen into was left behind.

LEARNING TO BUILD TRUST: SHIFTING DISTRUST TO TRUST

A Brief Note on Trust

Like other moods, we generally experience trust as an undifferentiated attitude about a person. We either trust them or we don't. But as discussed earlier, this automatic attitude or predisposition, is a mood that is connected to several related assessments:[49]

- Sincerity: The assessment that a person is sincere in her commitments. She does not make promises that she does not intend to fulfill. She does not have a secret agenda. She does not make promises inconsistent with what she is thinking.
- Competence: The assessment that a person is competent to deliver on his promise. A person could be sincere and well-intentioned but not competent to perform what is required.
- Reliability: The assessment that a person is able to fulfill her promises on a timely basis. A service provider, for example, is assessed as reliable when it regularly fulfills its promises, and manages its commitments to take care of its customers.
- Engagement/Care: The assessment that a person respects us, cares about listening to our concerns, and is committed to our well-being and to continuing to be in a relationship with us.

Every time a promise is made to us, we make an assessment of trust or distrust, and vice versa. Even if we don't make explicit assessments about these, they show up in other related moods that can negatively impact our ability to work as a team. For example:

- Distrust in the person's sincerity may show up as anxiety. "I am worried about our ability to succeed. She promised to prepare better for this

---

49 If you are interested in reading about this further, see Flores, *Conversations for Action and Related Essays*, Chapter 8. For more extensive reading on this topic, *see also* Robert Solomon and Fernando Flores, *Building Trust in Business, Politics, Relationships, and Life* (New York: Oxford UP, 2001).

Gloria P Flores

week's exercise, but since she has not done so in the past, why should I believe her now?" Or, "He promised to do something, but I have not heard from him for a while. I don't think he intends to follow through on his promise."

- Distrust of the person's competence may show up as resignation. "He has never done good work in this area and I expect that he will continue to perform poorly. Thus, we are unlikely to succeed in our project unless I do his work myself." Or in WEST, someone may say something like "the healer in our *World of Warcraft* team is not very effective at healing more than one player; there is no way we are going to be able to complete the dungeon."

- Distrust of a person's engagement with the team may show up as resignation or resentment. "I really want to succeed and achieve our objectives, but she puts absolutely no effort into learning her role. She does the bare minimum. She simply does not care, and because of her, we are going to fail. There is nothing I can do about that."

Ungrounded assessments of trust can open the possibility of big problems, including the failure of a project and the disintegration of a team. People who automatically distrust all promises, no matter who is making the promises, are unlikely to ever be partners with anyone – they will fail to make requests, and/or they will smother a person who made a promise to them with constant requests, inspections, requests for status reports, etc., thereby closing possibilities for both of them. On the other hand, people who accept all promises made to them may find themselves disappointed on a regular basis, since they trust people to perform who cannot be counted on.

When working with other people, many of us are somewhere in between, and at some point or another, we find ourselves in a mood of distrust. Our teams include people from different cultural backgrounds – which in today's world is inevitably true even when our teams are constituted entirely of people from our own countries – and different professional backgrounds. We have conflicting interpretations and different priorities. We have different standards

122

for what we deem appropriate or for what we think someone should do. And despite our desire to have relationships built on trust, trust breaks, and we fall into other moods that are not conducive to meeting our objectives, like resignation, resentment, anxiety, impatience, and frustration. Despite our objectives and initial desire to work together, our willingness to continue to collaborate begins to wane.

But if we are committed to working as a team, and to supporting each other to meet our objectives, it is precisely these moments that give us the opportunity to learn to build trust and also to learn from people who may show us things that we could not see for ourselves. Among different cultures, people will perceive things differently. "Easterners perceive things holistically, viewing objects as they are related to each other or in a context, whereas Westerners perceive them analytically and in isolation; Easterners use a wide-angle lens; Westerners use a narrow one with a sharper focus."[50] "The fact that cultures differ in perception, however, is not proof that one perceptual act is as good as the next, or that everything is relative when it comes to perception. Clearly some contexts call for a narrower angle of view, and some for a more wide-angle, holistic perception."[51] An engineer's focus on measurable results may be appropriate for evaluating the success of an initiative, but her marketing colleague's insistence that they also pay attention to the mood of their customers may be important as well if they are to retain them. If we are able to respect our differences and commit to building trust with one another, we are much more likely to be successful as a team.

We can choose to not allow ourselves to get derailed from building trust when the mood of distrust calls on us to give up. Just like we can strive to learn to navigate moods that keep us from our learning objectives, we can learn to build trust by exploring the assessments that may be triggering a mood of distrust. It is important to note that building trust requires that we

---

50 Doidge, *The Brain That Changes Itself*, 302.
51 Id., 303.

explore the mood of distrust that we find ourselves in, not for the sake of making a moral judgment about other members of our team, but rather for the sake of designing the actions we need to take to build trust and ensure the success of our team. For example, if we don't trust that a member of our team is competent to fulfill his role, what actions can we take to help him become more competent, and/or what actions can we take to fill in the gap that his lack of competence may leave for the team? As we explore our assessments together, and discover and clarify our standards if need be, we can then commit to new actions that will enable us to get on the same page, continue to collaborate to achieve our objectives, and build trust with each other, despite our differences.

Trust is a crucial aspect of teamwork and is constantly being evaluated. Here are two more examples emphasizing how participants developed their ability to build trust with one another during our Working Effectively in Small Teams course.

➤   Case Study #15: Learning to collaborate and to build trust
"I would never work with someone like that!"

(From distrust to commitment to building trust.)

In one of our courses, Tim, a manufacturing plant manager from the east coast was assigned to a team of five that included David, a software executive from Silicon Valley. Shortly after the course began, it became apparent that David and Tim did not get along. David tended to be short with Tim during the team's exercises. He got annoyed, particularly when Tim would take off in the game to explore on his own without telling the team. Tim thought that David was very uptight, and lacked flexibility to change course, particularly if it went against what he thought they needed to do. In private one-on-one conversations with us, both of them confessed that in real life, neither would ever want to work with the other. "I simply would never work with someone like that!" Daniel said. They were both resigned to the possibility of learning to collaborate with each another.

A couple of weeks into the course, an interesting situation arose.

The team agreed to meet at 4:30 pm EST on a Monday to complete that week's exercise. Unexpectedly, that morning Tim was asked to attend a quick meeting in mid-town Manhattan at 2:30, putting his ability to join the team on time at risk. He sent an e-mail to the team telling them that he was asked to be at a last-minute meeting, but that he was still hoping to get to their meeting. Not surprisingly, as Tim's work was a bit far from midtown, and it was rush hour, 4:30 came and went. The rest of the team showed up, waited for about 30 minutes, and then cancelled the meeting. David was upset and was more convinced than ever that he couldn't work with Tim. "What a jerk. He just can't be trusted to fulfill his promises." The team went off-line, and less than five minutes later, while members of the course delivery team were still online, Tim came on, and slightly out of breath, asked us where everyone was. He had worked his way through heavy traffic and literally ran to his office to get online and join the team. He was very surprised when he found that they had cancelled the meeting after waiting a half hour.

Shortly afterwards, David sent Tim an angry e-mail, copying the rest of the team and the delivery team. He accused Tim of wasting everyone's time and of not being a man of his word. He told him that as a result of not fulfilling his promise to his team, everyone had wasted time that they could have spent on other matters. In order to take care of the damage he had caused, David told Tim that it was up to him to coordinate with the team and to figure out when everyone could meet next. Tim was floored. "How dare he accuse me of not being a man of my word," he said to me. "I told them something un-expected came up but I was still hoping to make it. I fought traffic, I rushed back, and I ran back hoping to join them. I did my best." David said that Tim was unreliable and not trustworthy. Tim thought that David was a jerk who did not care about anyone but himself. And even though they were participating in the course to learn, among other things, to collaborate more effectively in teams, the possibility of them *wanting* to collaborate with each other was pretty small. In other words, even though in theory they wanted to learn to collaborate more effectively, they were not, in fact, open to collaborating with each other. They mutually disliked and distrusted each other, and that distrust was getting in the way of their learning to collaborate.

As we began to explore their lack of trust, they both began to see the assessments and standards that were getting in the way of collaboration.

David saw that his assessment of Tim's incompetence in this situation was based on his standard that "one must fulfill one's promise at all times." And as he explored that, he saw that we can't always fulfill our promises. Sometimes things come up that we do not expect, like Tim's unexpected meeting in Manhattan. This does not mean that promises are not important, but that if we can't fulfill them, we can still work together to handle the consequences of not fulfilling them. In this case, Tim could have requested that they reschedule or that they go on without him. But David saw that he could also have taken action to take care of Tim and the team as a whole. He admitted that he suspected that Tim would not make the meeting when he read the e-mail, but did not say anything. By not doing so, David could see that he was also responsible for the waste of time they suffered that afternoon. By not taking action, David also could see that he had waited for Tim to fail to make his promise so that he could have further evidence that Tim was not someone he would ever work with in real life.

Upon reflection, Tim also discovered that his standard for coordinating with people when unexpected circumstances arise was lacking, and could be adjusted to take better care of his team. He realized that simply giving people information did not tell them what to do. Tim told his team that something unexpected had come up, and that he hoped to still make it, but he did not tell them what to do if he did not make it on time. Should they wait for him? Should they proceed without him? Should they reschedule? Tim saw that in the future, informing the team that something has come up, and making a request or an offer regarding how to proceed, would better take care of the team and avoid the lack of coordination and the distrust that emerged that day.

After reflecting on this situation, the team resolved to take action that would help them work more effectively in the future and avoid such outcomes. By exploring their mutual distrust and the assessments that triggered it, they resolved to not stay in that mood and began to take actions to collaborate together. They agreed that they wanted to learn how to work together more effectively, and began to declare standards for the team, including what actions they would take if someone was late to a meeting or needed to miss it. After a few weeks of working together, Tim and David became much more open to working together. Although they do not need to collaborate in real life, they both left the course with a new appreciation of actions that they can take to build trust with their real-life teams so that when distrust first arises, they don't need to dwell in it and thereby abandon the possibility of collaborating effectively.

➤   Case Study #16: Learning to build trust by navigating away from distrust "Stop suffocating me with your offers of help."

(From distrust to trust.)

Amy, a trainer and coach who was taking the course for a second time, and Sarah, a non-profit executive, were assigned to a team with three other people, and much to Amy's surprise, they quickly found that they did not enjoy working with each other. The weekly team meetings were "not fun" and Amy entertained the idea of quitting the team. "I am so busy and I don't want to waste my time doing something that I am not enjoying. I have never had to work with someone like Sarah…"

Everything came to a head after one of the weekly team meetings. In this particular exercise, the team had to travel far (virtually, of course) to a new area in the game, an area that Amy was familiar with. As the team traveled, Sarah fell behind, and Amy asked the team to stop to wait for Sarah. "Are you okay, Sarah?" she asked. "Do you need help?" Sarah did not answer. After a few minutes, Amy asked Sarah again, "Can I help you?" and Sarah replied that she was fine. The team continued, but every so often, Amy said things like "Are you okay, Sarah?" or "How are you doing, Sarah?" Finally, Sarah had had enough of Amy's questions, and she loudly and firmly replied, "If I need your help, I will ask for it. Stop asking me if I need help! I really don't appreciate it!" Amy fell silent and did not utter another word for the remainder of the in-game part of the team exercise.

Upon debriefing the exercise, Amy and Sarah explored their assessments of each other and could see that they had fallen into a mood of distrust.[52]

Sarah to Amy: I didn't appreciate you hovering over me. You kept asking me if I needed help, as if I couldn't figure things out by myself. I felt micromanaged. You treated me like I could not be trusted. I don't like to work with people who don't trust me and feel a need to micromanage me.

Amy to Sarah: I was shocked by your reaction and did not think that it was appropriate at all. I felt that it was rude. I was simply trying to help you. I appreciate when people offer me help, and people have told me in the past that they appreciate me being aware of them and checking in with them. I was not trying to micromanage you. I simply was offering help if you wanted it. You made me feel like I did something wrong when I did not.

We continued to explore their assessments together.

Sarah: I felt suffocated by Amy. Her constant offers of help were being driven by her assessment that I am not competent enough to find my own way. She is offering to help me, but she is not taking care of my identity with the team.

---

52 This exchange is reconstructed from my notes. It is not a verbatim account of the conversation.

I don't want to be perceived as incompetent, particularly since I know that I can do this on my own. I don't need her help.

Amy: I think Sarah is questioning my motives for offering her help. I don't appreciate her questioning my motives and accusing me of doing something wrong. I simply wanted to help her. I don't have a secret agenda to make her look incompetent to team members.

Sarah reflected on her assessments of Amy's offer to help and realized that maybe she was misinterpreting Amy's motives. "I assumed that she was offering me help because she thought I was incompetent and could not figure things out on my own, and that she kept offering to help me because she wanted to look good and for me to look bad. I now see that she was simply offering help because she wanted to be helpful. She did not have a secret agenda." Sarah also saw that she had the standard that she had to be competent at all times, and if someone offered her help, she assumed they were assessing her as incompetent, which led her to feel defensive. She realized that with that standard, no one could ever offer her help, or if they did, she could never allow herself to accept it, and would end up always doing things by herself, depriving herself of a key benefit of being part of a team.

Amy reflected on her assessments as well. "I assume that people always want help and that they will be grateful if I help. I now see that maybe they don't always need help, or maybe they don't want it, and it is important to be aware of that. Otherwise, I will make offers that I think people will value, but instead they will just get annoyed with me. In turn, I will get annoyed with them."

In exploring the mood of distrust they found themselves in, Sarah and Amy realized that if they were going to be a part of a successful team together, they would need to build trust. They resolved to do so and began to explore new practices for working together. Sarah declared that she would not question Amy's motives when she offered help in the future, because she saw now that Amy did not have a secret agenda to make her look bad. She was going to assume that Amy is sincere in her intentions to help. Amy declared that she would be mindful not to offer constant help to Sarah, and asked Sarah to please ask for help if she wanted it instead. She also said that if she saw that Sarah needed help, she would still offer to help her, but that it would be okay with her if Sarah declined her offer. She would attempt to not be offended if Sarah says "I don't need help" to her like she had in the exercise. As a result of that conversation, Sarah, Amy, and the other team members kept these declarations in mind as they coordinated with one another, and they enjoyed working together much more.

LEARNING TO BUILD ELEMENTS OF EMOTIONAL FORTITUDE:

Cultivating Confidence in the Face of Uncertainty

When learning a new skill, we will encounter many moments when we don't know how to do something, either as a beginner or somewhere higher in the learning scale. Similarly, when facing new circumstances – new teams, new projects, new markets, new emerging technologies, new customers – we can expect to encounter many moments of uncertainty, when we won't know exactly what to do but need to take action and learn as we go. Yet, although we can understand this on paper, many of us don't embrace the new and the unknown as an opportunity to learn, to grow, and to invent new things with people. Instead of rejoicing because the unknown may open new opportunities for us, we fall into negative moods that shut down these possible opportunities, including some of the moods that have already been described:

> *Anxiety*: I don't know what to do here. I have to make a decision about which direction to commit to, and I have no idea what the right direction is. I am afraid my decision will lead us to failure. I may make mistakes and mistakes are bad. I may not recover from them. It's better to quit. It's better to not act because failing is worse than simply not trying.
>
> *Confusion*: I don't know what is going on here. I don't know what ⸝ do. Not knowing what to do is a bad thing. I don't like being ir situation. I need to get out of here.
>
> *Frustration*: I should know what to do, but I don't.
>
> *Resignation*: I don't know what to do and I am never go⸝ what to do.
>
> *Insecurity*: I don't know what to do. I can't do this. O⸝ than I am and they probably have a better idea o⸝ done.

If we find ourselves in these moods, we will b the unknown, and less open to take risks fᵣ with people in the WEST course over the past six years, we have worked with teams that became completely paralyzed in the face of uncertainty, some of which became irritated with us for not telling them "exactly" what to do and how to do it. They felt their lack of knowledge led to their failure, and since we had the knowledge they needed, it was our fault that they failed. In their quest for certainty, they failed to make decisions, experiment, and learn from mistakes, and they eventually ran out of time. Even though WEST's *World of Warcraft* exercises don't have anything to do with real life, the moods that many participants routinely fall into when faced with the unknown are real, and mimic the moods they fall into when faced with similar circumstances outside of the course. In this case, even though it would be no big deal for them to take risks and learn from their mistakes since their avatars can quickly come back to life, many of them don't. The moods they habitually and automatically fall into when faced with the unknown in real life show up for them here as well. Instead of embracing the unknown as a new adventure to conquer, they simply freeze.

In a world where uncertainty and rapid change are the norms, learning to cope with these kinds of conditions is important. To do so requires that we learn to navigate from the moods mentioned above and cultivate others instead, such as ambition, resolution, and self-confidence. By developing this skill, we can cultivate emotional dispositions that will imbue us with the will to embrace and engage with the unknown as an opportunity, not as something to fear and to avoid. How can we do this? Again, the process outlined in section 3 is helpful:

1) *Reflect on your learning objective.* Why do you want to learn to cultivate self-confidence in the face of uncertainty, for example? If you aspire to be an executive, perhaps you realize that you will often be in situations where you won't have all the answers, but you will still need to take action. People will look to you to make declarations about what to do, and not doing so is not acceptable for an executive. Freezing in the face of the unknown is not behavior that you will want to continue. As you reflect on this, you may start to become more ambitious

about learning to cope with uncertainty more effectively so that you can be an effective executive in an organization.

2) *Identify and explore the unproductive mood or moods that you find yourself in.* If you find yourself in moods of anxiety and insecurity, for example, what are the assessments that are operating in the background that may be triggering these moods? What are the standards underlying these assessments? For example, you may have the assessment that it is bad to not know exactly what to do ahead of time and that it is bad to make mistakes. Perhaps you also think that you should always be competent and that you should always have the right answer, and that people will judge you negatively if you don't. What are the past experiences that gave rise to these standards? Are these assessments well grounded? Are they conducive to you becoming more confident in the face of uncertainty? If you are in a situation where you are facing uncertainty, is it reasonable to demand absolute certainty before you act? Is absolute certainty even possible? If you spend all of your time preparing to act, and trying to anticipate everything that might happen or that could go wrong, will you get a chance to actually do so?

3) *Identify moods that are more conducive to reaching your learning objectives.* In this example, confidence and serenity are moods that would be more conducive to learning to cope with uncertainty.

4) *Speculate what action you could take to shift away from the unp*ductive moods and cultivate the more productive ones instea cultivate confidence, perhaps you can recall situations where v been successful in the past and situations where you we learn. How did you do it? If you were able to ask questir have surrounded yourself with the people who supr you do that again? Who can you ask for help? Do yr bers who have executed successful projects in th obstacles that they did not anticipate? What team? Are there people you can ask for ad· can take that will allow you to quickly lea· rective action when necessary? Perh-

pilot projects in unknown territory for the sake of quickly exploring new opportunities in a cautious manner, and for the sake of learning to cultivate a mood of self-confidence. As you explore possible actions to take, you may begin to see new opportunities for action that you want to pursue.

5) *Take Action.* Again, learning requires that you take action. Take the risk to do new things, to make mistakes, and to take action to recover and learn from them. The more you do this, the more confident you will become in the face of uncertainty, and the less likely you will be to get stuck in moods that prevent you from engaging when faced with the unknown.

➤ Case Study #17: Learning to take risks and to experiment in the face of uncertainty
"We can't jump unless we are absolutely certain that we can do so successfully."

(From anxiety about the unknown to confidence in the face of uncertainty.)

Working with a team of five again, composed of people from different geographies, backgrounds, and professions, we encountered a situation where the team discovered how extremely risk-averse they were, and how their fear of making mistakes led them to inaction.

In one of their last team assignments, we gave the team a surprise mission minutes before their meeting: They were to travel to a destination in unfamiliar territory. By now, the team had learned some rules in the game that ...ed them stay "safe" in the game, including the rule that it is generally ...to stay on roads so as to minimize the odds of getting attacked by bears, ...ogres, and other dangerous creatures along the way. In this case, however, ...is rule would not be too helpful for them because in the new, updated ...f the game, the road was broken and the only way to get across was ...om one cliff to another while riding their horses. If they jumped, we knew that they would either make it to the other side, or fall into the river be-low where they would be able to swim to the other side. It was highly unlikely that their avatars would die. But we did not tell them what we knew. They had to figure out how to accomplish the mission on their own.

Once they got to the broken road and saw that they were standing on a cliff with a river running below, they froze. One person said: "This can't be right. There is no road here." Another person said, "I am not comfortable jumping across. I don't know how to do that. We can't jump here." And a third team member said: "We know that the roads are safe and that it is better to travel on the roads. Let's go find another road." Although they could not make out any new roads on the map, they spent the next 20 minutes looking for a road that did not exist. They finally found themselves standing on the cliff above the river once again, wondering what they should do.

One of them tentatively suggested that it might be best to jump, but they all hesitated because they were not sure that they would succeed in doing so. Interestingly, prior to this exercise, this team had worked together five or six times, and they all knew quite a few things that could have influenced their actions here, things that they seemed to forget as they stood together at the edge of the cliff; they knew how to resurrect their avatars if they got killed, they knew how to swim, and they knew how to read a map in the game. Despite this knowledge, they spent a third of the time allotted for this exer-cise looking for a road that the map clearly did not show, and hesitated to jump for fear of falling into the water and dying. Finally, one of them noticed another player in the game – there are millions of people playing *World of Warcraft* all over the world – gallop past them on his horse and successfully jump. Actually, two other players had done that earlier, but the team hadn't noticed because they were so focused on trying to figure out a tried and true, familiar way to get to their destination. With only a few minutes left in their 90 minute-long exercise, they were inspired to jump and did so nervously. One by one they got across. A couple successfully jumped; a couple fell in the water but managed to swim across, quickly finding a way out of the water to rejoin the rest of the team. One fell into the water and got disoriented, and ended up getting out at the same place he had jumped from. After realizing this, he tried it again and succeeded in getting across to join the team.

They were elated. Although they did not get to the assigned destination before running out of time, after running in circles for over an hour they had finally succeeded in getting to the other side of the road, and they had learned to do something new. They learned that unlike in real life, in this game they could jump from one side of a cliff to another, and they discovered that it was okay to fall into a river because they could always get out. Of course, we could have told them this at the beginning of the exercise, but we did not, and subsequently, they fell into moods of confusion and anxiety. As they debriefed, they discovered two assessments that they had about the situation that impeded them from trying something new and from reaching their destination. They had the assessments that it is important to always be certain before you take action, and that it is bad to make mistakes.

Their fear of failure and discomfort with uncertainty closed off the possibility of taking risks, experimenting, and coming up with a successful strategy for action when they found themselves in a new situation, one in which the rule that they knew – stay on the road – was no longer applicable. Upon reflection, they reported feeling anxious because they did not know what to do and because they were afraid of taking action and being wrong. They saw that their lack of certainty temporarily paralyzed them and it took them much longer than necessary to finally get across.

As a result of this exercise, they resolved to explore how to cultivate confidence in their teams and in themselves when faced with new or changing circumstances. In this case, they saw that they might have been able to reduce their anxiety and could have built confidence sooner simply by reminding themselves that they had experience swimming and resurrecting their avatars, and hence falling in the river was really no big deal. They were pleased to find out that another team had experienced the same paralysis, but unlike them, did not jump prior to running out the time allotted for the exercise. Instead they spent the whole time looking for another road. One of them said: "At least we are not the *most* risk-averse team in the course." They were not, but they came close. Other teams, who had generally the same experience in the game as this team, did not hesitate to jump, and successfully arrived at the assigned destination within the allotted time. The main difference between this team and the teams that succeeded was their emotional disposition towards the unknown. When standing at the cliff, the general mood of the successful teams was confidence, both in their ability to recover quickly if their avatars died, and in their ability to work together and to help each other out if one of them got lost or did not know what to do. Often members of these teams said things like, "Remember to call out if you are lost or under attack. Let's have fun! Let's go!" In other words, stuff may happen, and if it does, we will work together to get through it.

➤ Case Study #18: Learning to cultivate confidence and serenity in the face of the unknown
"The more knowledge I have, the more control I have. I try to anticipate everything and spend a lot of time preparing. But I hold my breath the whole time in fear that I might have missed something."

(From anxiety and overwhelm to confidence.)

Joshua, an IT Consultant, was a member of a team that tended to spend a lot of time preparing for their weekly team missions in *World of Warcraft*. Joshua proposed -- and most of the team happily accepted -- that the team create alternative "practice" avatars to execute the weekly assigned missions prior to meeting with a member of our staff to complete their assignment with their course avatars.[53] As soon as we posted the homework assignments, Joshua

---

53 The other team member, Carmen, a bank vice-president, also accepted, but later admitted that she was not happy because she really did not have the time to spend doing extra hours of work in the course, hours that our team did not require them to do. She did not say anything about it though, and it ended up providing her with good insights as to why she did not feel comfortable saying "no" or making another counteroffer. Similarly to Beth in the case study above, Carmen resolved to begin to practice making these moves in the future.

would read what we were requesting each team to do in the game and do some research on the Internet to prepare himself and the team. The team would then meet, and would often stay online until they completed the assigned mission, even if it took longer than the time that we gave them for that particular assignment. Afterwards, they met with a member of our team to complete the assignment with their course avatars.

Not surprisingly, when the team met with us, they finished the exercises in record time, without much conversation. Joshua had helped the team prepare, and during the exercise he simply reminded his team members what to do. The debriefs were uneventful. At first, they were happy about their success, but after the second and third time, they were starting to get a bit bored, and wondered what they were learning.

"What would you like to learn?" I asked

"To coordinate better, to be more confident in handling new situations. That is why I signed up for this course. It is great that we practice a lot, and that Joshua helps us prepare so well, but in real life, I don't have a Joshua. I don't have someone telling me what to do." Carmen, the person who had not been happy about the extra practices they had agreed to do as a team, replied. "My work involves a lot of unknowns. I am stressed most of the time, and if I can learn something that helps me with that, I'd be happy."

"The way I handle uncertainty," said Joshua "is to try to anticipate everything. The more knowledge I have, the more in control I feel."

"Are you able to anticipate everything that might come up in your projects?" I asked.

"I try. I spend many hours worrying about everything. I work very long hours trying to ensure that nothing will go wrong. Then, I hold my breath. I am totally stressed until the project is over," Joshua replied. "I am so stressed that I often find myself daydreaming about quitting and retiring to live in nature."

After talking about this a bit more, all of them could see that during the course, and in their real lives, they routinely fell into moods of overwhelm and anxiety, triggered by the following kinds of assessments:

Overwhelm: There is so much to do and so much that could go wrong. There is nothing I can do except work harder, try to anticipate everything that could come up or that could go wrong, and since chances are I will miss something or something will go wrong, I am afraid we may not be successful anyway despite all of my efforts.

Anxiety: We don't know what we are doing. We have no idea how to play this game and complete the assignments that are given to us. Unless we really prepare, plan everything we do carefully, practice by completing the assignments on our own ahead of time, we are going to fail. Failing is bad.

As they became aware of the moods they found themselves in, they resolved that they wanted to learn to cultivate moods of confidence and serenity about their work instead.[54] They wanted to be less fearful of the unknown, and more confident in their ability to cope and thrive in it. We recommended that they practice less as a team in between their weekly sessions and that they not complete the team assignments we gave them ahead of time with their practice avatars. They agreed, but not wanting to take any chances given Joshua's tendency to do a lot of research ahead of time, minutes before they were supposed to meet with us, we changed their assigned mission, and gave them a new one, so that Joshua would not be tempted to spend a lot of time preparing prior to their meeting.

After a few minutes of confusion and discomfort, the team began to coordinate. They discussed what we were asking them to do, and got on the

---

54 See section III above for other sample assessments giving rise to these moods. In this particular situation, confidence could mean trust in the team's ability to work together, to learn together, and to make adjustments as necessary. Serenity here could mean accepting that they can't anticipate everything that is going to happen and that unanticipated things may come their way, including mistakes, but that's a normal part of life, and they can recover and learn from it.

same page about what they had to complete in order for their mission to be deemed successful. They went over their respective roles. They declared that they would stay together as they traveled in the game, a practice that they had previously adopted and that they assessed had worked well for them. They reminded themselves of the "fight formation" should they come under enemy attack, a practice that they had adopted previously, and that they agreed to continue in this practice exercise. If anyone felt lost, s/he was asked to say so immediately so they could take care of him or her, and they did. They ran into trouble a few times, but they were able to pause, make assessments about what was going on, what was working and not working for them, and made adjustments accordingly. When time ran out, they had not quite completed the entire mission, but they came really close. If they only had a few more minutes, they would have prevailed.

When asked to reflect on his mood at the end of the exercise, Joshua replied that he was in a mood of confidence about the team and much more serene than he had been in previous exercises. He found that he was not worried about what might go wrong. He said that even though we did not allow them to do any planning ahead of time, they all knew their respective roles, they had practices that they had adopted in previous exercises that worked well in this one, and when they ran into trouble, they were able to make assessments and come up with strategies that worked. "I am less afraid to make mistakes with this team now because I know that if we do, we can talk about it and figure out how to recover."

Interestingly, Joshua felt more "in control" during an exercise that he was not prepared for than during the previous exercises he had spent a lot of time preparing for. "I feel like a weight has been lifted off my shoulders." Other team members shared similar observations. Consequently, they became ambitious about continuing to practice coping with uncertainty so that they could learn to cultivate confidence and serenity in their real lives as well, and resolved to continue to do their weekly exercises without practicing as a team ahead of time.

7

Conclusion

OTHER ENVIRONMENTS FOR LEARNING TO LEARN

We can begin developing the skill of learning to learn at a very young age by encouraging children to experiment, to take risks, and to make mistakes. Schools can play an important role in cultivating this ability. However, it is important to keep in mind that even young children will make assessments that are not productive to their learning based on experiences they have already had and standards that they have adopted that guide what they judge as appropriate or inappropriate behavior. In the example about one of my sons mentioned above, my son fell into a mood of resignation about the possibility of excelling at math because at some point he was not fast enough at understanding some problems, and he concluded, therefore, that he was not smart. In his case, I can't imagine that any of his teachers ever told him that to be smart he had to be fast, but somehow he judged that getting something slowly, rather than right away, meant that math was not his cup of tea. Had we not explored the assessments he had that triggered his mood of resignation, he might not be pursuing a science major today. His younger brother also had a learning stumbling block at the ripe age of 5. We noticed that he always claimed to know everything. Apparently this is not uncommon; I am often told: "My son/daughter/sister is just the same!" Whenever we tried to explain something new to him, he always interrupted us and would say that he already knew that. Almost every time, if not every time, his siblings, father, or I tried to help him do something new or teach him something, he stopped listening and quickly stated, "Oh yeah. I know that!"

We thought it was amusing at first, and his brothers began to call him "IKnowThat.Com."[55] However, as time went on, I noticed that he did not listen very well and I even got his hearing checked. (His hearing was perfectly fine. His listening was another story!) For some reason, perhaps because he is the youngest of three boys, he thought it was very important to look like he knew everything. Looking at the common assessments that people make that get in the way of learning, I could see that even at five years old, my son thought that it was important to always know everything, and not okay to admit that he did not know something. After many conversations in which we focused on showing him that not only was it okay not to know, it was good not to know, because we then can discover something new, our youngest began to be more comfortable not knowing, and his nickname, Iknowthat. com, became a funny anecdote about his younger years, and is no longer descriptive of his behavior today – for the most part. Teenage years are fast approaching though, and I expect the nickname to be applicable once again.

We cannot avoid falling into unproductive moods that may block our learning, but we can learn not to be trapped by them. If we take them seriously, unproductive moods are a great window for discovering expectations or standards for behavior that we may have adopted in the past that may not serve us to learn in our present situation. If teachers and other mentors learn to help their students identify unproductive moods, explore the assessments that may be triggering those moods for them, discover standards that they may be adhering to that may be detrimental to their ability to continue learning, and enable them to cultivate more productive moods instead, they will make a great contribution to their students' ability to learn to learn on an ongoing basis. Unfortunately, sometimes, unaware of the impact of their words, educators – teachers, other mentors, and parents alike – help to cultivate unproductive moods instead.

---

55 After baptizing their younger brother with the Iknowthat.com nickname, we discovered that it was also the name of an education site that my kids ended up enjoying for quite a while.

As a parent, and someone who has been around many people as they strive to learn new skills, I have seen and heard about many situations where unintentionally, I am sure, a teacher helped to cultivate moods that are not conducive to learning.[56] For example, when one of my sons was in fourth grade, he fell into numerous moods that were unproductive to learning to write a five-paragraph essay, an essay where young children for the first time in their lives have to write with a certain structure: an introductory paragraph with a thesis statement, three paragraphs that support the thesis, and a conclusion. My son, up to that point, loved writing and was very good at writing short creative stories and poems. When it came to writing a five-paragraph essay, however, I saw him in the following moods:

Confusion: I have no idea what I'm supposed to do. I don't know what my teacher wants. I don't understand why she says what I am doing is bad.

Frustration: I should know how to do this. My teacher expects me to do better, but for some reason, I can't. My essays are bad.

Resignation: My last essay was bad. I did poorly on the written part of the test. I am never going to learn to do this.

Insecurity: I am bad at this. Other kids seem to know what to do. I am stupid.

Similar to his older brother, prior to this event, school had been fairly easy for him. He enjoyed it, his teachers complimented him, and he did well on all subjects. It was a surprise to both him and to me when his new teacher – a teacher who he had had for three weeks – told us that she was concerned about his learning ability because his essays were "really very bad" and that "he should be doing a much better job than he is by now." She thought that we should think about having him tested for a reading disorder. None of his other teachers had ever mentioned any concerns to me, his most recent end of year test placed him in the "advanced" category for Language Arts, and

---

56 Of course, teachers are not the only ones who can unwittingly help to cultivate unproductive moods sometimes. As parents, we are often guilty of that too.

I had not noticed any learning difficulties myself. My heart began to beat a bit faster and I became worried that maybe I had missed something. As we talked, it became clear to me that my son did not know how to write a five-paragraph essay, and that up to that point in his schooling, he had never had to do that. He transferred into this class late, and I was not sure how much instruction he had received about how to write these essays. Clearly, his teacher expected him to know how to write those essays at that point and was concerned about him. To make a long story short, over the course of the next couple of months, my son painfully struggled through his writing assignments. He brought home short essays and told me that his teacher told him that they were bad, and that he needed to redo them at home. I asked him what instructions or feedback the teacher had given him. "Nothing." I'd take a deep breath, knowing what would unfold during the next few hours: Lots of suffering for him and comments like the ones mentioned above. "I am stupid. There is something wrong with me. I can't do this! I am a bad writer. I can't understand what I am supposed to do." He would spend over an hour dreading what he had to do before he could even start attempting to do it. He was convinced that he was not a good writer and that he would never be a good writer. But, little by little, his confidence in his ability to learn grew. Using the Dreyfus scale of learning model, we talked a bit about what happens when someone is a beginner at something, and how confusing and frustrating it can be, particularly if we think that we "should know" how to do it, or if others think we should know how to do it. In this case, he began to see that there was no reason for him to know how to do this kind of essay yet, as he had not been taught how to do it. We talked about the structure of a paragraph. We talked about thesis statements, supporting evidence, and conclusions. He was able to see that he usually had something interesting to say, and that he simply did not know the rules for saying it in the format that his teacher required. Eventually, he learned to write a basic five-paragraph essay, and his teacher told him that she was proud of him. He gained confidence and no longer felt that he was not capable of learning. He was placed in honors English in high school, but, interestingly to me, this is the subject matter where he still tends to fall into self-doubt most often and the subject where my husband and I are most alert to helping him cultivate self-confidence whenever necessary. Becoming aware of our children's moods, and helping them learn to shift unproductive moods and cultivate moods that are conducive to their ongoing learning, is, to me, just as important as teaching them the multiplication tables.

Besides school, learning environments such as the one we developed for our Working Effectively in Small Teams program can be an effective use of technology as means to reinforce the cultivation of these skills in a fun and playful manner. If you have not yet mastered these skills as adults, it is not too late. As the work that we have done in the WEST course demonstrates, you can start learning to learn the moment you decide to embark on that journey, and it is a journey worth making, because you will find that learning to learn will enable you to learn any other skills that you want to acquire.

LEARNING TO LEARN TO BEING OPEN TO THE WORLD AROUND US

Learning to learn is perhaps one of the most important skills that one can develop. In a world of constant change, where what we learn today may be outdated in a few years, the ability to learn and acquire new skills is paramount. While we can all agree with this statement, most of us don't know what we can do to develop this skill. We've seen in this book that a crucial aspect of learning to learn is cultivating a disposition that opens us up to learning. This inevitably requires letting go of assessments that may hinder our capacity to learn and block us from learning. These assessments are based on standards that we have adopted over the course of our lives that may have been useful in some situations – and may still be – but that don't serve us in the process of learning something new. We often discover the standards that we have developed, often unconsciously, by becoming aware of our moods. There are certain moods that systematically close off the opportunity to learn if we are not vigilant, but there are others that we can learn to cultivate that will predispose us to learning on an ongoing basis.

Learning is not a one-time event, but a continuous process. Using the Dreyfus model for the acquisition of skills, we can see that a person will be able to perform different things depending on his or her level of mastery of a particular skill. A beginner follows rules and asks questions; an expert, given her vast repertoire of experiences, will quickly see how to achieve a goal without thinking of the rules or procedures to follow, and so forth. It is important to keep in mind, however, that a person will experience different moods at each of these stages as well, and will regularly fall into moods that are not conducive to continued learning. This is part of the learning process. If we are to continue learning and to reach our learning objectives, we must learn to be aware of the moods that we find ourselves in, and learn to take action to shift moods when necessary if we find that we have fallen into moods that are not conducive to our goals.

Learning to observe our moods, and to explore the assessments and standards that may be triggering them is a skill that can only be learned by doing. This requires putting ourselves in situations where we experience a roller coaster of moods, and commit to take actions that will allow us to shift moods that get in the way of learning.

Real life is a wonderful laboratory for learning, but depending on the skills that you are trying to develop, it may feel scary, if not dangerous, to practice taking risks and making mistakes there. Understandably, if we are developing our skills for leadership, for building trust, for engaging in more candid and productive conversations with people, we may be reluctant to use our work environment as a learning laboratory. There we run the risk of offending the wrong person or making mistakes that may be hard to recover from, and all in the name of practice. Nevertheless, it is important to always keep in mind that learning requires practice, and if we are to meet our learning objectives, we must look for ways to prudently take risks to do so, starting with people who we can trust at work and in other areas of our lives.

In addition, we have found that game environments are helpful for learning these kinds of skills. As the case studies in sections 5 and 6 of this book show, we have found that when you situate a real team in a virtual reality game environment, provide players with a rich framework for observing how they work together, spaces for reflection and for guided practice, these skills can be developed in a fun, low-risk manner. By providing an environment in which people are asked to engage with others, practice, take risks and make mistakes, reflect and discuss, over and over again, we have found that people not only learn new skills for collaboration, but they do so by learning to learn, a skill that makes the successful acquisition of the other skills much more possible. With such a skill, not knowing what to do does not show up as a problem, but rather as an opportunity to learn and to grow; with such a skill, we are much more predisposed to be open to the world around us, enhancing our capacity to expand our world and enrich our relationships; and with such a skill, we are much less likely to fear the unknown, including each other.

Bibliography

Argyris, Chris. "Teaching Smart People How to Learn." *Harvard Business Review* May-June 1991.

Badal, Sangeeta Bharadwaj, and Bryant Ott. "Delegating: A Huge Management Challenge for Entrepreneurs." *Gallup Business Journal* 14 Apr. 2015.

http://www.gallup.com/businessjournal/182414/delegating-huge-management-challenge-entrepreneurs.aspx.

Davidson, Kate. "Employers Find 'Soft Skills' Like Critical Thinking in Short Supply." *The Wall Street Journal*. Wsj.com, 30 Aug. 2016. http://www.wsj.com/articles/employers-find-soft-skills-like-critical-thinking-in-short-supply-1472549400.

Davidson, Richard J., and Sharon Begley. *The Emotional Life of Your Brain: How Its Unique Patterns Affect the Way You Think, Feel, and Live—and How You Can Change Them.* New York: Plume, 2012.

Doidge, Norman. *The Brain That Changes Itself: Stories of Personal Triumph from the Frontiers of Brain Science.* Penguin Books, 2007.

Dreyfus, Hubert L. *On the Internet.* London: Routledge, 2001.

Dreyfus, Stuart E. and Dreyfus, Hubert L. *A Five-Stage Model of the Mental Activities Involved in Direct Skill Acquisition.* Rep. U of California, Berkeley. Operations Research Center, 1980.

———. *Beyond Expertise: Some Preliminary Thoughts on Mastery.* Published in *A Qualitative Stance.* Ed. Klaus Nielsen. Aarhus UP, 2008. 113-24.

Dweck, Carol S. *Mindset: The New Psychology of Success.* New York: Random House, 2006.

Ekman, Paul, and Richard J. Davidson. *The Nature of Emotion: Fundamental Questions*. New York: Oxford UP, 1994.

Ekman, Paul. *Emotional Awareness: Overcoming the Obstacles to Psychological Balance and Compassion: A Conversation between the Dalai Lama and Paul Ekman, Ph.D.* New York: Holt Paperback, 2008.

Flores, Fernando. *Conversations for Action and Collected Essays: Instilling a Culture of Commitment in Working Relationships*. Ed. Maria Flores Letelier. CreateSpace Independent Platform, 2012.

Friedman, Thomas L. "How to Get a Job at Google." *The New York Times*. 22 Feb. 2014.http://www.nytimes.com/2014/02/23/opinion/sunday/friedman-how-to-get-a-job-at-google.html

———. "Learning to Keep Learning." *The New York Times*. 13 Dec. 2006. http://www.nytimes.com/2006/12/13/opinion/13friedman.html

———. *The World Is Flat: A Brief History of the Twenty-First Century*. New York: Farrar, Straus and Giroux, 2005.

The Future of Jobs: Employment, Skills and Workforce Strategy for the Fourth Industrial Revolution. Rep. World Economic Forum, January 2016. Global Challenge Insight Report.

Goleman, Daniel. *Destructive Emotions: How Can We Overcome Them?: A Scientific Dialogue with the Dalai Lama*. New York: Bantam, 2003.

Groysberg, Boris. "Keep Learning Once You Hit the C-Suite." *Harvard Business Review*. Nov. 2014. http://hbr.org/2014/06/keep-learning-once-you-hit-the-c-suite

Hansen, Randall S., and Katharine Hansen. "What Do Employers *Really* Want? Top Skills and Values Employers Seek from Job-Seekers." *Quintessential*

Careers. Aug. 2008. http://www.physics.emory.edu/faculty/roth/career-skills/soft_skills.pdf

Heidegger, Martin. *Being and Time*. New York: Harper and Row. 1962

Hoskins, Bryony, and Ulf Fredriksson. *Learning to Learn: What Is It and Can It Be Measured?* Rep. Office for Official Publications of the European Communities, 2008. JRC Scientific and Technical Reports.

Nikias, C.L. Max. "What Will the Future of Education Look Like?" *World Economic Forum*. 23 Jan. 2015. http://www.weforum.org/agenda/2015/01/what-will-the-future-of-education-look-like/

Ricci, Mary Cay. *Mindsets in the Classroom: Building a Culture of Success and Student Achievement in Schools*. Prufrock Press, 2013.

Solomon, Robert C., and Fernando Flores. *Building Trust in Business, Politics, Relationships, and Life*. New York: Oxford UP, 2001.

Stansbury, Meris. "Ten Skills Every Student Should Learn." *eSchool News*. 11 Aug. 2011. http://eschoolnews.com/2011/08/11/ten-skills-every-student-should-learn/.

Syed, Matthew. *Black Box Thinking: Why Most People Never Learn from Their Mistakes – But Some Do*. New York: Portfolio Penguin, 2016.

Torkington, Simon. "The Jobs of the Future – and Two Skills You Need to Get Them." World Economic Forum. 2 Sep. 2016. https://www.weforum.org/agenda/2016/09/jobs-of-future-and-skills-you-need.

Winograd, Terry A., and Fernando Flores. *Understanding Computers and Cognition: A New Foundation for Design*. Norwood, NJ: Ablex Publ., 1987.

About the Author

Gloria is co-founder of Pluralistic Networks and is committed to developing innovative ways for people to learn to collaborate, build trust, and build value for each other. Of particular interest to her is how the world of multi-player on line role playing games can be enhanced and cultivated as environments for developing new skills.

As a consultant, trainer and coach, Gloria has focused not only on bottom line results, but also on the development of skills for individuals and teams that enhance efficiency, flexibility and customer satisfaction while creating a style of care and innovation. Gloria has a BS in Business Administration from UC Berkeley, and a JD from Cornell Law School. She lives in Oakland, California with her husband and sons.

CPSIA information can be obtained
at www.ICGtesting.com
Printed in the USA
BVOW04s1217271217
503778BV00005BA/68/P